Self-Esteem
Gift from God

D1490231

Practical, insightful, and extremely helpful are just a few of the words that describe Ruth Ward's book. Basing her writing upon the Myers-Briggs Type Indicator, the author has made these principles come alive for anyone reading this book. Many people struggle throughout their lives to accept who they are. By discovering the fact that God has designed us in a special way will help anyone delight in who they are and thank God for their unique expression.

As you read this book, you will probably find yourself not only saying, "That's me," but eventually proclaiming, "It's alright to be the way I am; I'm God's creation." As you discover more about yourself through Ruth Ward's writing, you will find new and positive ways of relating to others in your family, at work, and at church.

—Norman Wright

Self-Esteem
Gift from God

RUTH M^cROBERTS WARD

SMYTH&HELWYS
PUBLISHING, INCORPORATED • MACON, GEORGIA

SMYTH&
HELWYS

Smyth & Helwys Publishing, Inc.
6316 Peake Road
Macon, Georgia 31210-3960
1-800-747-3016
© 2000 by Smyth & Helwys Publishing
All rights reserved.
Printed in the United States of America.

The paper used in this publication meets the minimum
requirements of American National Standard for Information
Sciences—Permanence of Paper for Printed Library Materials.

Library of Congress Cataloging-in- Publication Data

Ward, Ruth McRoberts
    Self-esteem: gift from God / Ruth McRoberts Ward.
        p. cm.
    Includes bibliographical references.
    ISBN 1-57312-313-7 (alk. paper)
    1. Self-esteem—Religious aspects—Christianity.
    2. Myers-Briggs Type Indicator. I. Title

BV4647.S43 W37 2000
155.2—dc21   00-041026

Illustrations by Dean Vavak

To Mac,
my middle brother,
who has been my lifelong friend and encourager,
and who introduced me to the Myers-Briggs Indicator

Many people know Mac as Chaplain Marvin McRoberts,
U.S. Army. Now retired from the Army, Mac is Chaplain of
the Northeast Methodist Hospital, San Antonio, Texas.

By helping people better understand how God created each of us with distinct personalities, Ruth Ward brings us to a greater appreciation and acceptance of who we are. Applying insights and applications from the Myers-Briggs Personality Inventory, Ruth enables us not only to accept ourselves but also to better understand others who are different from us. Her engaging and readable style, interesting stories and illustrations, and keen insights make *Self-Esteem: Gift from God* a book you will find very enjoyable and encouraging and will want to recommend to others.

—*David C. Waltz*
Executive Director-Treasurer
Baptist Convention of Pennsylvania/South Jersey

Ruth Ward's book shows us that to reject ourselves is to reject the gift of God's design for us. She underlines the important fact that nobody is a nobody and that self-esteem is a developmental task for every stage of life. *Self-Esteem: Gift from God* is not a quick fix that encourages self-centeredness; rather, it uncovers types of personality traits and helps each of us discover how we fit in the mosaic God has designed. It offers an understanding of other personality types that helps us know how to build relationships rather than tear them down.

—*Johnnie C. Godwin*
Author and Publishing Consultant
Nashville, Tennessee

Contents

Preface

When I was 49, I wrote *Self-Esteem—Gift from God* to put temperament information in the language of laypersons. Now, 16 years later, I hope that it has real merit for helping people accept who and how they and others are. For the last several years that *Self-Esteem* has been out of print, I've had numerous requests for the book, even though I've covered different aspects of temperament in other books, namely, *Blending Temperaments: Improving Relationships—Yours and Others* and *Coaching Kids: Practical Tips for Effective Communication.*

I write because as a counselor I can't interview everyone I'd like to help. One of the most significant experiences of the ministry of *Self-Esteem* occurred in 1995 when a single woman in her late 30s wrote, "If what you say in *Self-Esteem* is accurate, then I'm not crazy like my family says." My affirming reply prompted an exchange of monthly letters and the discovery of a fascinating, brilliant person who lay buried in her culture. We enjoy a special postal and e-mail friendship. She graciously contributed her experience for this preface:

> I was given *Self-Esteem—Gift from God* for Christmas 1994, and a whole new world opened up to me. Until then I had the mistaken idea that there was one ideal model the lives of all Christians should fit. This book introduced me to the notion that God designed at least 16 different models for His children. INTP fit me very comfortably.
>
> I learned that INTPs are especially talented at objective analytical abstract thought, and that this enabled us to think of ingenious solutions for complicated and complex problems that most people considered impossible to solve.
>
> I was raised in the world of manual labor (Old Order Mennonite) and expected to enjoy it and to succeed in it. It bored me to death. After learning my type, with its strengths and weaknesses, the Lord led me step by step to the world of abstract thought applied to real life for the concrete

and constructive improvement of people's lives, which I find very satisfying. In short, the book *Self-Esteem—Gift from God* started me on the road of learning who I am.

This gal with only an eighth-grade education—all her culture allows—has cautiously and without her church's or family's approval entered the university on probation, getting to classes via her horse and buggy and wearing plain clothing. Her professors are astounded by her competitive "A" work. She's finally been released to pursue what God has equipped her to be capable of achieving. She's a brand new person learning to balance herself and relate to people as she lives in one culture and studies in another.

Recently I became acquainted with a 20-year-old college freshman who was struggling with her relationship with her mother. I gave her my loan copy of *Self-Esteem*. She had taken the Myers-Briggs Temperament Indicator (MBTI) elsewhere and knew her letters. She wrote:

So I knew my letters were ENFJ, which means I'm extroverted, intuitive, feeling, and structured. I never fully understood how this made me work or interact with others. Then I read *Self-Esteem—Gift from God*, and it gave me a positive outlook on my unique characteristics. It impressed upon me that I am made in God's image, so it's okay to love myself just the way He designed me.

This book has also given me a greater appreciation for others, especially my mom. I've always felt that unless I did things her way, they were not good enough. After reading *Self-Esteem*, I understood my mother's "sensing, hands-on arena" much better. She takes pride in cleaning the house. As a mind-on intuitive, I take pride in learning, reading, or thinking about a new idea that holds little interest for her. I've learned that this only makes her different, not inferior.

With the knowledge of opposite preferences I was also able to appreciate my friends more than ever. When it dawned on me that one of my closest friends is an introvert, I began giving her more space. She burns out quickly if she can't have time alone. A guy friendship took a major turn when I realized he thinks one thought at a time while I juggle several. He is spontaneous, and I am structured. When he calls me the night before to make plans for the next day, I tend to panic. I used suggestions from the book to make us both happy. The book wonderfully illustrates your particular personality on a bike ride. Immediately, you know which person you are on that journey, and you can begin to enjoy the ride with ease. I wish everyone was required to read the *Self-Esteem* book!

A 34-year-old single man said after learning about his temperament: "I wasted so many years because I didn't know who I was supposed to be. I'm like no one in my family, and they've all tried to make me change. We run a family business, and I operate in the future while they all operate in the today. Now I know I'm normal—just very different. This will help us survive together."

Considering these personal accounts and all the requests for the book, I surmised, "*Self-Esteem* is still viable, still helping people right on the spot. I wonder if there's a publisher who would have faith in the ministry of this book?" How delighted I was when Smyth & Helwys stepped up to the plate.

Acknowledgments

I wish to express appreciation to several persons for their help. Thanks to:

- My pastor friend, Paul Broyles, and to Ken Lyle who kept encouraging me to get *Self-Esteem* back in print.

- Lynn Clayton, an editor and author himself, who 33 years ago discovered my flare for writing and risked our friendship by correcting my first article with a red pencil; broke my heart but taught me not to be afraid of editors.

- Johnnie Godwin who, with years of experience in writing and with a kind heart, picked up where Lynn left off and counseled and encouraged my early writing.

- Linda McFarland who, in wanting to protect my already crowded counseling, teaching, and speaking schedule, took a tremendous load off my mind by keying the new edition onto computer disk.

- My Sunday morning Bible study group, Wednesday morning Bible study, Wednesday night discussion group, and Sunday night personality study group where we've discussed temperament from every angle. They have all encouraged, challenged, supported, and held me up in prayer.

- My daughter, Kay Baldwin, who participated in the verbal birth of ideas on our daily walks.

- My dear husband/partner of 45 years, Jim, who understands when I'm in another world—the intuitive one—and lends his steady, dependable, and loving support.

Introduction

"The turning point in my life came when I discovered my personality type—that who I was was OK. I was finally released to like myself and show others the love I felt for them."

—A 40-year-old mother

"I've never lived out just what I am or think, but always what I thought someone expected me to be. I have a new life ahead."

—A 37-year-old alcoholic father

"Knowing I'm normal and like a few others really relieves me."

—An elementary-school teacher

"I'm not really lazy, then, am I, just because I put things off?"

—A 30-year-old father

"Our family is finally pulling together."

—A wife and mother

God only makes somebodies, but the world takes God's somebodies and tries to make nobodies out of them. Every person is valuable; no matter how worthless certain ones feel. In addition to the necessities of life—food, shelter, and clothing—everyone needs a sense of dignity and worth that will provide context for the maturing of their personalities.

Low self-esteem is at the bottom of most misunderstanding, jealousy, depression, marital breakups, child abuse, guilt, lethargy, drinking, weight problems, and many more social hang-ups. The world is full of good people who feel inadequate, inferior, and apologetic for taking up oxygen and space, and who either excuse themselves or try to change their inborn way of perceiving and acting or else, in their insecurity, attempt to force others to be just like them.

Contrary to what society seems to believe, God didn't make all males identical and females just alike. Instead, God created a number of unique designs where many men and women possess basically the same preferences. This causes confusion and problems as well as challenges. When people understand and appreciate their own particular set of temperament preferences, much personal and social pressure, guilt, hurt feelings, and disappointing expectations will be modified or completely eliminated. In their place, self-esteem will be raised for all involved.

Learning who and what we are, by God's design, takes the apologies out of life. We become more confident and satisfied with who we are and are not, realizing that God has made us different, even from someone we may admire and wish to be like. It's nice to know who we are so we can deal with ourselves.

Knowing about temperaments also helps us learn that there are men and women in the world who are similar to ourselves. We have probably already picked them out, but have not known what attracted us to them.

Healthy self-esteem releases us to be as God designed and also fosters open and honest communication in the home, church, and neighborhood. Knowing our temperaments can facilitate career choice and avoid wasted time and money. It can also aid in mate selection and adjustment to marriage. Few marriages are incompatible—just lacking in understanding.

When congregations and businesses utilize temperament analysis, committee, leadership, and job placements are wiser. Teachers who understand temperament types can make education a new adventure, meaningful and fair for every student.

Self-Esteem—Gift from God should help readers accept and appreciate themselves and gain new respect for their spouses, family members, friends, and co-workers. Healthy self-esteem, an inborn gift from God, paves the way for each of us to become rightly related to the Creator and to communicate with Him. It also prepares us to join hands with God, using the potential of our gifts to fulfill God's dream and goal—that of spreading the good news.

. . . Living well is hard work!

[For the sake of confidentiality, names and situations have been changed.]

Chapter 1

Self-Esteem—
Its Worth and Sources

Favor is better than silver or gold.
—Proverbs 22:1b

I began writing this manuscript on my birthday. No, I don't mind telling—May 7, and because birthdays and age figure into self-esteem, I have no reservations about revealing that I'm 49. This year's celebration made me keenly aware of the recharge for self-esteem that comes tucked into cards and notes. Some samples will help identify one source of self-esteem and alert you to this simple but valuable way of lifting the spirits of others.

Thank you for blessing our lives. We praise the Lord for you.

Love,
Bill, Diane, Nicole, Michael

I can't tell you how much your friendship means to me. I truly appreciate our time together. God has blessed my life through you.

Love,
Sharon

You have helped us so much. Praise God for the wisdom He gives you to give to others.

Love,
Dave and Donna

I want to thank you for your love, prayers, and good counsel.
A Friend

You certainly are faithful with your letters to Mother; she thinks you walk on water.

Janie

Hopefully from the life and beauty of the butterfly and flowers on the card, you may get a vision and a feeling of what I am thinking and feeling about you today. Have a very happy birthday all year long. Looking forward to seeing you soon.

John

I hope you are having a great year and getting your wonderful thoughts on paper so all of us can be blessed. Remember, you are very special to me.

Sincerely,
Nell

I cannot put a price tag on these gifts. They are heartwarming! The first card was handpainted and signed individually by each family member. That note not only encouraged me, but also provided an opportunity for me to thank the children—ages 5 and 8—along with their parents. Thus, their self-esteem was raised by knowing they contributed to mine. The card from Janie, my older sister, whom I've always idolized, meant so much. Because I admire her greatly, her written approval and recognition of my worth increased my self-esteem. Then, the little note that John, my oldest brother, inscribed on a carefully chosen card just made my day! I felt ten feet tall. John is very important to me, and it pleased me to know I am important to him.

Because my self-esteem gets such a healthy boost every May when I receive written approval and positive feedback, you can understand why I don't mind acknowledging those years. However, this ample supply of encouragement won't last until I'm 50. I'll need a constant trickle from other sources every day, as everyone does.

This more-than-adequate supply of encouragement and support in the form of birthday cards and notes inspired me into writing action. A belated card and note from an out-of-state friend, Nell, gave me extra incentive to produce. The confidence of others urges me on. But even though most self-esteem hinges on the opinions of others, it cannot take root unless my own appraisal allows me to accept their evaluation.

Potential sources of self-esteem are not always easily identified, and thus not appreciated. In fact, much quality self-esteem is never realized, understood, or utilized until we are much older. According to psychiatrists, self-actualization usually does not take place until a person reaches age 50. What a pity! It doesn't have to be that way.

"Confidence comes from knowing who you are and what you can do," says a 21-year-old who has been brought up on appreciating himself even before he has chosen his career. He has been accepted as he is. How has such a young fellow beat the average self-actualization statistics? Let's start at the beginning by analyzing the definition of self-esteem.

Definition

Self-esteem is a little-understood, abstract quality that influences and controls our entire existence. Many people recoil at the word, thinking it is egotistical and self-seeking. Instead, they prefer to demean themselves in an effort to avoid being conceited, which only produces negative results.

Our need for self-esteem resembles the need of the body for iron. While the need is absolute and daily and the sources many, the intake is often of little concern and sporadic, if not neglected entirely. When we're low on iron, we become draggy, tired, run-down, and anemic.

People who have low self-esteem compensate by taking drugs or alcohol. However, that kind of emotional boost is short-lived and carries many negative side effects. Others attempt to drown their feelings of inadequacy with activities or possessions and often become depressed by these empty, expensive pursuits. Others choose lifestyles that reflect loss of self-respect.

Webster states simply that self-esteem is "confidence and satisfaction in oneself." Pride is a sense of our own proper dignity or value. It is self-respect, pleasure, or satisfaction taken in our work, achievements, or possessions. Self-esteem is beneficial.

Self-respect is not to be confused with egotism, which Webster describes as "the practice of speaking or writing of oneself in excess." It involves an inordinately large sense of self-importance.

Egotism resembles the "upper" one takes—a sort of shortcut to feeling good about oneself. An excessively high opinion of self is conceit or arrogance. Proverbs 16:18 warns that "pride goes before destruction, and a haughty spirit before a fall."

Persons who have an ego problem think they are the source of their own abilities. Some strive to satisfy their ego by seeking status, thinking the only way to be accepted is to be prominent. But prominence is so fluid, based on what a person wants out of someone else, that one cannot depend on it.

Those people who know how valuable they are do not have to talk about it, and yet one's self-respect colors how one perceives his or her importance to others. So, our assignment is to discover how to balance these two attitudes. We don't want to put ourselves down, yet we don't want to lift ourselves up too high. The key lies in discovering how God designed us, understanding our strengths, appreciating our weaknesses, and learning to accept others as God made them.

Sources

Self-esteem, like iron, is subtly all around us and rather elusive at times. We just have to discover its sources and how to extract it. Self-esteem is something I have not always had in abundance because my poor self-image, or self-doubt, prevented natural sources from taking solid root. Since we do not outgrow the need for self-esteem and cannot store up a lifetime supply, I want to trace the worth and sources of self-esteem by using the information I know best—my own trek of discovery in the hope that I can help others understand and appreciate their reason for being.

A couple of traumatic experiences that happened when I was nearly 15 sparked my self-esteem to life and growth. But before that I was pretty low on this quality. However, because by God's design I am naturally confident and optimistic, for many years I was able to camouflage my inner low opinion of my worth.

Many successful adults hide their poor self-image all their lives, evidencing it only in the way others are disrespected and ill-treated. I was 25 before I became comfortable with my personality and potential.

Marriage and family counseling with hundreds of clients has revealed how common this poor-image bit is and how enormous is the need for understanding and for acquiring self-esteem. Marriage and family relationships, especially, are needlessly marred through ignorance. Raise the self-esteem in couples, and watch marriage, family, school, and business conflicts make smooth transition toward wise compromises.

Black Sheep Blues

Although I was one of six children in an average American rural home, between the ages of 12 and 14, I remember many times sitting on the porch gazing into the moonlit night and wondering who cared for me and whether anyone—preferably a male—ever would. I was lonely and sad, a misfit. I didn't like myself at that young age, nor did many others, in my opinion. I'm not sure whether I was actually called the "black sheep" of the family or whether I just assumed the title because I was an awkward middle child, but I fit the pattern.

I didn't get along with my brothers and sisters or friends very well or for very long at a time, or even with my sweet, quiet, overworked mother. My dad seemed to appreciate—even favor—me, but he traveled all week, and weekends provided scant attention.

I toyed with the idea of running away just to test whether or not anyone would miss me, but I didn't have enough self-confidence to risk that venture. I was convinced I had no significance—couldn't play the piano, cook, paint, sew, or draw. I hated to work alone. My only fame was being in the middle of every conflict—negative fame.

I suspect that my grandparents tolerated me for a week every summer because they wanted to give my mother a break, though I did feel special when I visited. However, I always felt intimidated and inferior in most every way when a more self-confident cousin was present.

I even yearned for the day when I would be recognized for saying something significant or funny—like my sister Jane. Nothing I said seemed important or amusing. I just felt transparent, bland, unneeded, and unwanted. My presence made no difference.

I can recall the first time the family actually laughed at something I said. We were returning from church—eight of us crowded into a Hudson sedan—when my oldest sister, Shirley, wondered aloud why they dragged the hymns out so. "Probably to help the old women who can't see the words clearly to keep up," I replied. Everyone laughed, and I felt warmly fulfilled and accepted—like I belonged.

Being starved for approval and recognition is a common, healthy appetite that some children feel more than others. If children are not served self-esteem, they learn to grab it wherever they can.

Because we are social beings and dependent on others for a supply of approval and attention, when we don't get what we need—even after we grasp for it—we tend to withdraw in self-doubt, which only intensifies the problems. This was my 12-to-14-year-old dilemma.

Family

Although I felt unloved and unappreciated as a quality member of my family, I can now spot, in retrospect, sources of healthy self-esteem, which I hope will enable young parents to be more sensitive to their children's unspoken, unidentified needs. Although growth in self-esteem begins at birth, one cannot recall all the contributing factors.

As a rural 1940s family, we listened to the radio, sang around the piano—Daddy played—pored over picture puzzles, played cards—I was proudly Daddy's partner—ate popcorn, and enjoyed soft drinks. We played softball, picnicked, gardened, canned, visited grandparents, attended church and movies and fairs, played with neighbors, shot fireworks, and entertained soldiers from a nearby air base.

We three middle children—two brothers and myself—expelled most of our boisterous energy by doing outdoor chores; playing marbles, tag, basketball, football, cops and robbers; having snowball battles; riding bikes; and exploring the woods. We romped through the two-story farmhouse throwing knotted socks (when Mom and Dad were gone) and argued over table games, played ping-pong, and boxed. Many a bloody nose I got. I certainly wasn't a delicate lady.

Corporate family relationships feed self-esteem by insuring that each person is part of a larger group. I belonged, whether or not anyone, including myself, liked it.

Parents. I received a big dose of self-esteem when my mother reminisced how special I had been to Dad as a baby. He had named me—after her—and was the only one who could stop my infant crying. Daddy's lap was certainly my special domain. Although he was usually reading rather than paying attention to me, I snuggled in security and acceptance. In a way, I drew on him in desperation for importance. Maybe Dad didn't really favor me—my brothers and sisters don't recall that I was his favorite. Perhaps it was the other way around—I favored him. Whichever way it was, I pulled affection and attention from that big guy. I thought he was the smartest, handsomest, most able man in the world. I wanted to marry someone just like him.

Some of my most satisfying memories are of accompanying him on local business calls—little ego trips, actually. I pretended to be his secretary. I remember sitting so prim and proper next to him on a couch, too sophisticated to play with a client's daughter. We'd eat lunch out. He'd buy me little packaged cookies, a special treat to a country child.

My father showed me how important I was by bringing me pecan rolls or a new dress after his weeklong trips. Naturally, I'd meet him at the door no matter what time he arrived home. That must have frustrated Mother, but she never scolded me for barging in on her time. I don't think the other children were aware of his special gifts to me—probably because I didn't want to share my candy (I kept it a secret).

Daddy paid me royally, and secretly, for shining his shoes and doing other favors. He responded to my tears when I'd beg to go with him and Mom to neighborhood adult get-togethers.

Although she found me a very difficult child, my dear mother encouraged self-esteem by giving me and the other children a daily list of chores, which were sources of accomplishment. She gave me personal time each morning when she braided my long, thick hair. Although we didn't have the dialogue I longed for, I now know why.

Mom was always home when we returned from school. How much that added to our security and feeling of importance! Snacks of cookies and milk would be on the table along with individual lists of chores. She refrained from degrading name-calling, though she called us brats at times. I don't blame her. We *were* brats! I'm sure she called me lazy, which is true of many children, and I certainly was no exception.

Siblings. I trace much of my early self-esteem to my brother Mac, who is 16 months younger than I. For years we were constant companions, nearly like twins. We climbed trees, roamed the woods, played in the creek, rode bikes, worked in the garden, killed and plucked chickens, teased our little brother David, gathered eggs, and reluctantly assisted Mother in paring fruit, picking and preparing vegetables, and washing jars for canning. We designed our own games and rarely tired of one another. We seldom disagreed.

Mac and I rarely were apart until he reached preteen age and began to view rough-and-tough John as a more challenging playmate. John, who is three years older than I, found that keeping his younger, noisy, sensitive sister in tears was a great sport, to which Mac lent some support. In spite of the traumatic change and rejection, I had already received his approval.

I understand now that John was in the same pickle as I—alone in a crowd because our two older sisters were companions, and Mac and I stuck together. The baby was seven years behind me. When Mac joined John's team, however, I compensated by creating Janet Johnson, an imaginary friend. I had to have someone in the lonely country situation. Janet liked me and accepted me totally. Naturally, we got along beautifully! She and I were college mates involved in helping imaginary people solve problems. We skated the long, cracked, and windy walks that spindled out from the four porches on our secret missions. John and Mac teased me mercilessly when they overheard my private conversations with Janet. But to a degree, even negative attention contributes to self-esteem. To be ignored is the worst treatment.

A bonus boost came unexpectedly one afternoon. John, Mac, and I were riding bikes a mile from home, and mine developed a flat tire. John, with whom I fought constantly and often declared in fits of rage that I hated, instructed me to ride his bike home while he walked mine. It was an expression of love and protection that I'll never forget, one that proved I was important to him.

Siblings can be very cruel, strategically attacking the most vulnerable areas by name-calling. What one is called as a child sticks like glue. My long teeth gave me the name of "buck teeth," and strong athletic legs earned me the titles of "piano legs" and "Amazon woman." Even though long, thick braids were my only beauty asset, criticism that my hair was straight as a stick and a horrible dishwater blonde cut me deeply. Anything connected with dishwater had to be bad! However, those negative comments were neutralized when a dear lady at church, who often gave me gifts and attention, marveled in the presence of several people about my beautiful hair and its lovely color. I beamed for a week. Youngsters do hear what adults say. I was starved for a compliment. How I wished it could have been my personality, instead, for which I was praised.

One mistake I made was insisting that Mother allow me to have my hair cut before I was old enough to take care of it. Then, it was short and straight as a straw—unmanageable. But my sisters, both older, did their part to let me know how important I was by taking time to converse, to curl my hair occasionally, and to sew pretty clothes for me. My older sister, Shirley, had a pet name for me—Fis—which I loved to hear, but neither of us have any idea how it came to be or what it meant, but her tone was accepting. Being seven years older than I, she especially took up for me when I was little.

One of my favorite memories as a six-year-old is the bicycle wreck Shirley and I shared. I was riding on the back fender when my brand new shoe got caught in the spokes, causing us to go sprawling on the pavement. I received coveted attention from a minor injury to my arm, but no reprimand regarding the shoe. I had previously ruined a pair of shoes while breaking ice in the creek, so there I was, treading on thin ice again. But the best part was that no one blamed me.

Self-esteem came to me every birthday, although I always feared they'd forget because I didn't feel worthy of a celebration. But as if by magic, my favorite cake would appear, and gaily-wrapped presents would be hidden near the table. Family celebration is so important—for me, anyway. Birthdays represent my unique day of the year. In fact, I have two birthdays.

One boring day I happened to be rummaging through Mother's small cedar chest of private papers when I discovered my birth certificate. What a find! A legal paper with my name on it, proof that I belonged. It paid to be nosey! On closer scrutiny, however, there appeared to be a discrepancy because the certificate recorded my date of birth as May 7, not May 5, which I had observed for 11 years. I was in a quandary. Who was right—Mother or that little piece of paper? I realized that finding out for sure would disclose my snooping. I normally avoided confession, but I took the risk.

"Oh, Ruthie," Mother said nonchalantly, "we must have gotten yours and Mac's dates mixed up. His birthday must be the 5th of September instead of the 7th." So, with little to-do, Mac and I reluctantly switched days. He was really disappointed, too, because his old birthday often fell on the first day of school, which had made it extra special. I've always felt a little guilty for spoiling his fun. So, for my 12th birthday I waited two days longer until the 7th to celebrate. It took some time to get used to the new day; in fact, my brothers and sisters still send cards on the 5th, which makes it unique in another way—a family day and a public day.

We learned later—20 years later to be accurate—when for military reasons Mac sent for his birth certificate, that his birth really did occur on the 7th. So, he got his old date back after all. However, his sacrifice had already been made.

I've marveled many times since at Mother's wisdom in not sermonizing me for violating her privacy. I wonder today how insecure children like myself manage more serious news—that they either were not wanted or that their father is not who they always thought. By comparison, my problem was plain vanilla; besides, I've had barrels of fun telling that birthday story.

School

School was my favorite arena, even though I had difficulty getting along with my peers. Teachers liked me because I loved learning and always completed homework thoroughly and ahead of time. When the superintendent of schools made his monthly visit to our three-room elementary school, the teacher always called on me to read aloud, which not only relieved the other kids considerably, but also was a feather in the teacher's bonnet and served my self-esteem.

And I'll never forget the day when, as an 8th-grader, I was selected to substitute as teacher for the 1st graders. That greatly spurred my self-confidence and fed my self-esteem. The unhappiest day of the year was the last day of school. How I dreaded it!

But even with all that family/school encouragement, I still thought I was no good—worthless! And that's just the time when the bottom really fell out.

The Worst and Best of Times

Mother had a stricken look on her face when we came in from school one Friday. "Daddy won't be home tonight," she said quietly. She showed us a note she had received from him in the mail that day. "Going south—see you in two weeks." He had enclosed a check for a hundred dollars.

"He won't be back," she said softly. "What do you mean, he won't be back? The note says he'll see us in two weeks," I pleaded. "I just know he won't be back," she said sadly. I guess she understood Daddy better than we children did.

John, 16 and the eldest son, went out to get a bucket of coal. Mac, who was 13, began his studies. Our little brother, David, who was 6, was too young to understand. I was 14 and totally confused.

I didn't want to believe Mother. Certainly she was wrong. If Daddy had left, why didn't he take me? I was his favorite. I didn't sleep much that night. Instead, I watched the road for the headlights of his car. They never came. I was crushed. That was my very worst day.

I was very lonely. The two older girls, already through school, worked in a nearby city. Being the third daughter, I had always slept alone at the end of the hall or in the sewing room. Even though we kids played and worked together, we fought a lot, and it seemed I was always in the middle.

Mother was much too busy with all the canning, cleaning a 10-room home, and caring for her large family to notice me much. Since Daddy traveled, she bore the burden alone most of the time. I also had difficulty making and keeping friends at school, so I enjoyed having my make-believe friend who was always nice to me.

I had lived for Daddy's Friday night returns. Sometimes they would be two weeks apart. I would watch the country road for hours for the headlights of his car. I nearly always beat Mother to the door. However, that happiness would last for only a couple of days, and Daddy would be gone again.

This time Daddy had, indeed, deserted us. My world caved in. He was the most important person in my life. What would I do? What would we do? Our house was out in the country, and we had no car and no money. The problems seemed insurmountable.

After school on Monday I was surprised to find my aunt and uncle visiting. Evidently they had been there most of the day. Nothing was said, but after they left, Mother seemed deep in thought—as if she were in another world. We could tell that something was going on—a strange feeling, a heavy atmosphere, almost as if a death had occurred —but no one said anything.

We began to have devotions each night after supper. That was new. I had never read the Bible or had spiritual thoughts before. We read a written prayer at the end of the devotion, and I always felt foolish when it was my turn to read.

Christmas was different that year. There was no money to buy presents, but that didn't matter too much, since we didn't have a way to get to town. Daddy had always brought piles of things for each of us. No one apologized for the lack, though my two sisters did pool their checks, and we had some semblance of Christmas.

Then we learned that we would be moving to Mother's small hometown. Daddy must not be coming back for sure. Weeks had passed; I still grieved. The little church we attended took up an offering, and friends brought soup and other needed items on moving day.

How shocked we were to pull up in front of a tiny three-room, paintless shack and learn that it was to be our home—with 10 rooms of furniture! There was no inside toilet, not even running water in the house. Impossible!

Mac and I just watched it all happen. We didn't ask questions, and no one apologized or explained what was going on. We had complete confidence in Mother's decision. The house, which belonged to Grandma, was to have been torn down and a new one built, but we lived in it rent-free for eight years.

We struggled to decide which furniture to keep. What about the piano? There was barely enough room for us kids. But we eventually crammed in the necessary things, including the piano, dog, and cat.

Then things really began to change. Although we were extremely crowded, my second-oldest sister, 18 years old, came home to assist Mother. Our aunt and uncle who lived nearby got busy in another way. They led Jane to the Lord. Right before our eyes, like magic, her life changed, and she began reading the Bible. Then they talked with John. He, too, accepted Christ. His life and conversations changed. We had always called him "Sonny Bear" because he was grumpy in the morning, but now he got up singing. Amazing! Mac and I just observed.

Soon after that, Jane and John confronted Mac and me with the claims of Christ. Although we had always attended church and Sunday school, we had never heard the gospel before. They told us that Jesus loved us, died for us, and wanted to be our personal friend. I figured I could surely use a friend. They told us that only those who accepted him would spend eternity in heaven.

We both made dry-eyed decisions. That was the best day of my life— close on the heels of the worst day. I lost my Daddy, my best friend, but in less than a month I found Jesus. My worst day paved the way to the best day of my whole life. From that day until this, I have experienced a wonderful, unique, growing friendship with Jesus, and he has given me many precious friends.

Conclusion

My story is not much different from yours. Many modern families are still too busy to notice and deal positively with a bratty, but needy and insecure child. I believe that hunger for self-esteem propels children to get into trouble at home and at school. They're seeking self-esteem that comes from getting attention or approval—negatively or positively. Unfortunately, many people do not learn positive ways.

This hunger, which resembles selfishness, is carried over into marriage and parenting where it produces misunderstanding and lack of appreciation and encouragement and prevents the growth of good communication. That's why we have drug addicts, criminals, alcoholics, suicides, rescue mission crowds, unwed mothers, prostitutes, divorces, and on and on.

The sources of self-esteem are our parents, siblings, neighbors, friends, achievements, and opinions of ourselves. The doses come in varying degrees and quality as we and others become aware of this necessary ingredient of mental health. Much self-esteem is nurtured by family and friends, but these sources are not reliable because we don't always live near our families and friends. People who are riding exclusively on parents, family, and peers are in for a fall when parents die and friends move away or become preoccupied. Achievements, prestige, possessions, and money do not adequately satisfy either.

Some counselors have dealt with this dilemma by attempting to reason a person into self-esteem. Impossible! Though their goals are worthy and encouragement often induces immediate confidence, such suggestions frequently border on egotism—self-centered "me-ism," or navel-gazing—which is short-lived as far as a permanent solution goes. Me-ism does not alleviate problems that develop from lack of positive feedback from people.

When we learn positive ways to get self-esteem, real maturity and happiness result. And when we discover the pure source of inexhaustible self-esteem—God's approval, attention, encouragement, and unique gifts to each of us—we have the beginning of deep-seated peace and confidence, which not only equips us to cope with put-downs, slights, and attempts to undermine our judgment, but also, and more importantly, helps us to appreciate ourselves and to elicit our supply of people- based self-esteem.

Most people are not aware of God's unique packaging. Every person possesses built-in esteem provisions that God designed to form a constant, ironclad, bottomless reservoir. Understanding our design and also having a personal friendship with our Creator thoroughly equips and releases us to utilize and enjoy to the fullest our God-given strengths, to understand our weaknesses, and to encourage others. We can then enjoy being God's co-workers in sharing God's love with the world.

Father, thank you for family, friends, and teachers who help us discover ourselves. Thank you for using every event in our lives redemptively

Chapter 2

How Bad Is Inadequate?

But who indeed are you, a human being, to argue with God? Will what is molded say to the one who molds it, "Why have you made me like this?" Has the potter no right over the clay, to make out of the same lump one object for special use and another for ordinary use?

—Romans 9:20-21

"It's so very nice to meet you," I said when introduced to an attractive elderly lady. She responded, "I'm just an old lady."

"You don't look like an old lady," I comforted. "Your skin is wrinkle-free, and your hairdo is becoming."

"But I can't walk very well," she broke in, "and I have this hearing aid, I guess they told you. I'm not really much good to anyone anymore."

"Well, you certainly have a nice smile," I remarked with sincerity, "and your eyes are bright and sparkly."

She looked at me inquisitively and said, "I just don't know what to say when someone says good things about me. It makes me feel funny and embarrasses me."

Everyone needs positive feedback, and often it keeps us going. All of us have much to share with others. This woman, along with millions of others, needlessly suffers from critical inadequacy.

Listen to Julie, a young married woman who phoned one morning in near hysteria: "My mother called and accused me of being distant. What's wrong with me?" she wailed. "I feel guilty and inadequate because I'm not pleasing my mother. I'm so aware of myself; I'm not concerned about others. I'm selfish. I used to listen and care."

A teenager asking advice wrote: "I am 16 years old and just plain ugly. My hair is flat, my nose is enormous, my lips are too thick, my skin is oily, I'm too skinny, and I wear a size 9 shoe. Don't tell me looks don't matter. I hear that a lot—from people who look like [model] Cheryl Tiegs. When I meet someone new, I try to become transparent and say nothing. I am afraid to call attention to myself. Then they think I am stupid on top of being ugly. I need help."

Men often suffer from low self-esteem, too. George, a 40-year-old father of teenagers, whose marriage was crumbling, said, "In order to have friends, I've never lived out just what I am or think, but always what I thought someone expected me to be." Going along with the crowd does not increase self-esteem, but rather weakens it. Layoffs and unemployment in recent years have uncovered many hidden male inadequacies. When these men admit their low opinion of their worth, their wives lose confidence, and I'm sorry to say, respect and trust. Often these men seek out the bar and the bottle for friendship and comfort.

Counselors hear many accounts of inadequacy. All of us want people to like us, agree with us, approve of us, and desire to be around us. When these longings are not fulfilled in marriage, home, and place of employment, we often consider ourselves inadequate. Self-esteem plummets, crippling our positive contributions to society and often causing mental distress that leads to a whole network of problems.

Inadequate means "insufficient, not able, incapable." Often our desire to measure up, to meet the standards, to improve performance, or to count for something degenerates into nervousness and fear of failure, as in Betty's case:

> I was assigned to the computer. I was nervous because it was something new to learn. I was afraid I couldn't learn it as fast as the others. I was afraid the office crew would laugh at me. I feared embarrassment. I was also afraid I would cry if I failed—I look terrible when I cry. I felt that anyone else could do a better job.

This experience nearly triggered a nervous breakdown. People work hard to hide indications of being unable, unstable, or not measuring up, fearing others' negative impressions and rejections. Hunger for positive feedback about ourselves is normal because the opinions of others affect our self-confidence. When yearnings to be important to someone, capable, productive, and competent are not realized, most people feel inadequate. And how bad is inadequate?

Most inadequacy feelings stem from normal human differences in temperament. Many people believe that their personalities are flawed when they observe those who are more assertive and outgoing, or can grasp ideas and instructions more quickly, or are more accurate or have keener concentrations, or are physically more attractive, or have more self-control.

Some people envy those who have creative ideas or the ability to figure out complex mechanical or people problems. Others dislike the fact that their verbal responses move slowly and heavily. Many despise their quick tongues. Some may feel inadequate because they are not as organized. Still others may not enjoy doing the things or filling the roles that society has relegated to a particular sex. All these "I'm nots" add up to feelings of inferiority.

Below is a list of inadequacy feelings I have heard expressed over the years in counseling sessions. This list pinpoints so-called inferiorities in a helpful way. Place a check by those with which you identify.

- ❏ My production doesn't measure up to that of others.
- ❏ I say things I don't mean.
- ❏ I'm unable to express myself clearly.
- ❏ I'm depressed much of the time.
- ❏ I wear my feelings on my sleeve.
- ❏ My personality falls below the norm.
- ❏ My public performance leaves much to be desired.
- ❏ My personal appearance is far from attractive.
- ❏ I'm grossly overweight.
- ❏ My nose is too prominent.
- ❏ My legs are short and stubby.
- ❏ My home isn't as luxurious as my sister's.
- ❏ I always think the worst about everything.
- ❏ I start more things than I can finish.
- ❏ I can't delegate responsibility.
- ❏ I dislike housework.
- ❏ I never know what to say.
- ❏ Children make me nervous.

- ❏ I can't lead—only follow.
- ❏ I have no self-discipline.
- ❏ My work is shoddy.
- ❏ I'm irresponsible.
- ❏ I forget appointments.
- ❏ My verbal contribution is inferior and of little impact.
- ❏ I'm forever losing things.
- ❏ I can't remember things, names, and such.
- ❏ I can't work as fast as others.
- ❏ I speak before my mind is in gear.
- ❏ I can't tolerate error in myself or others.
- ❏ My education is insufficient.
- ❏ I get discouraged easily.
- ❏ I teeter between constant struggle and failure.
- ❏ I have to run in order to keep up.
- ❏ The things I want to do, I don't do.
- ❏ The attitudes I don't want to have, I seem to have.
- ❏ My parents didn't want me.

❏ My Dad said I'd never amount to anything. He's right!

❏ I've made dumb mistakes.

❏ I'm unhappy in my job.

❏ My children have messed up their lives.

❏ My spouse is not as intelligent as my friends' spouses.

❏ My family's reputation is a drawback.

❏ I'm divorced.

❏ I have nothing to show for taking up space and oxygen.

❏ I'm single; no one wants me.

❏ I have to work so hard just to pass.

On and on these beratings go. When we look up to certain people— idolize, envy, admire them—comparing ourselves with them tends to leave us feeling inadequate. We have difficulty evaluating ourselves because we know the inside story of our struggles to accomplish.

Until we accept the truth that God did not make a mistake when He made us and that on purpose God did not make us all alike with the same abilities and gifts, we cannot appreciate our unique potential or that of anyone else. What we see as inadequacy in ourselves may be regarded as a plus or a benefit by others, but we usually want what we don't have. As someone said, the grass on the other side always looks greener—but that grass has to be mowed, too.

In reality, one's so-called inferiority is another's strength and vice versa. "Inadequate" is primarily a figment of our imagination and can be erased by changing our thinking. By the time you finish reading this book, your self-esteem should have increased greatly, and understanding and appreciation of others should also have soared.

In discussion with one couple who had made their personal evaluations after reading a book on temperament types, the wife didn't want to reveal hers. Her husband insisted that she couldn't even decide what she was, that he knew her better than she knew herself, and therefore had determined for her. "Tell them what you are, Sonja," he urged. Finally, with head down, she groaned, "I'm melancholy. I wish I had never found out what I am." What a shame! She was completely unaware of her strength of character, independence, ability to function in a crisis, and to concentrate. Thus, their study on temperaments made him stronger and her weaker. Knowing your temperament should be a boost in morale rather than a put-down.

The self-help books that encourage us to love, understand, and protect ourselves are good as far as they go, but unless we learn how to appreciate and understand others, our world will be a little warped.

Although each person is unique because of genetic heritage and environmental influences, another set of identifiers has emerged through the Myers-Briggs Type Indicator.[1] Using this technique with my family, church groups, and friends and in marriage counseling has raised self-esteem and generated the appreciation and encouragement on which effective communication depends. The following testimonies will demonstrate:

"You mean it's alright for me to be like I am?"

—A soft-spoken young mother

"Knowing my type has been like a feather in my cap."

—A male truck driver

"It's wonderful to feel good about myself and to understand myself. It makes it easier for the Lord to use me to help others. I know that I still have a lot of growing to do, but it's more fun learning now."

—A single seminarian

"We've both been aware of our differences, especially in decision making, and rather than using the differences together to make strong decisions, we've tended to use them against each other to make weak ones. Usually our decisions have been unilateral, even though we'd discuss the issue. Hopefully we can use our differences constructively now that we have the analysis. We need to heed what we are for each other, and that calls for lifestyle adjustments difficult to make."

—A pastor and his wife

"The relationship between my son and husband has improved enormously. My husband is now actively trying to help Pete find and afford a different school. To each of us individually the Myers-Briggs analysis has helped us see ourselves as we really are. It has brought a great many things into focus, things that before were just in the back of our minds but never really thought about deeply. Pete's attitude toward himself and his Dad has become more positive and relaxed. We are really making an effort to be more understanding and tolerant of each other."

—The mother of a college-age son

"Recently I realized that God made me a certain way, even down to my private preferences, and that I wasn't just a result of incapabilities, inadequacies, and underachievements. God has given me certain strengths and weaknesses that are unique and important. Learning this helped me appreciate myself more and certainly upgraded my opinion of others. They, too, are a unique blend of personality preferences. When I understood this, I didn't merely tolerate people anymore, but appreciated them for their differences and found I could enjoy anyone's company better.

"Now I see how God made me with capabilities to do certain things well, and I no longer put myself down for not being able to achieve in certain areas as others can. I have sharpened my aim at goal setting, too, and have a better idea of the kind of job I should choose. My inborn need to be with people tells me I should not work in a place where I am isolated from them. I also realized that I get satisfaction out of making things with my hands, so that's an area I will aim to improve in.

"My opinion of myself has gone up since I realized God designed me in a certain way to perform certain tasks. I allow others to excel in their preferred areas without envy or criticism, which results in a certain satisfaction knowing that my goal isn't to be like them.

"The Body, made up of many members, is more complex than I imagined and also more ingeniously designed so that everyone has a multitude of reasons to be like himself and others."

—A 23-year-old

Isabel Briggs Myers, who is responsible for the temperament typing, received her inspiration from her mother, Katherine Briggs, who applied the principles of Jung's *Psychological Types* during Isabel's childhood.[2] She in turn carried on the experiments with many of her friends, her own children, and thousands of high school and college students in the 1960s. This means a 50-year span to formulate testing based on psychological type.

The Myers-Briggs Temperament Indicator is the most widely used personality measure for the nonpsychotic population. Myers notes,

The merit of the theory . . . is that it enables us to expect specific personality differences in particular people and to cope with the people and the differences in a constructive way. Briefly, the theory is that much seemingly chance variation in human behavior is not due to chance; it is in fact the logical result of a few basic, observable differences in mental functioning.[3]

The Myers-Briggs Temperament Indicator has proven to be quite accurate for hundreds with whom I've worked. In almost every case, people have received help. The information is not really new, but it moves personal evaluation from the realm of subjective opinion to one of objective facts.

A single person in her late 30s surmised: "Funny how we have to have the things we already know or suspect defined for us. Then we are comfortable with them and assured. I am a brand new person. Where once my differences produced guilt and shame because other people gave the impression that I should feel that way, now I think 'phooey on what you think, I'm proud of how I am.' "

Conclusion

As I have done in other books, I'm using a well-known activity as an aid in making clear application of the truths we discover. Imagine that we are all involved in a bicycle trip. The time for departure has been announced. A sweeping observation reveals that the majority of bicycles are shiny, late model 10-speeds, equipped with comfortable sturdy seats, large baskets, horns, reflectors, generator lights, nifty handle grips, speedometer, odometer, compass, and rider bars on the back fenders.

A smaller number of bikes are not particularly striking in appearance or the latest models, and these are equipped with only minimal accessories. Many bikes even have rusty and bent fenders. However, most of these bikes have odometers, and several have small baskets and riders' bars.

The participants' attire and gear are just as varied. Most of the bicyclists carry cameras, lunch boxes, water jugs, transistor radios, first-aid and repair kits, detailed maps, report books, and rain wear. A smaller number carry binoculars, nature guides, notebooks and pens, psychology books, bags for possible finds, and a few general directions. Three-fourths of the travelers' jackets bear insignias of groups or organizations, while personal identification emblazons the rest.

As in all group trips, some people arrive long before departure and busily make adjustments, inventory supplies, and compare their watches, eager to leave as soon as the sun comes up. Others are right on time. Another group straggles in a little late, still rubbing sleep from their eyes.

All of us are part of this group of bicyclists, whether or not we recognize ourselves. We will rely on this trip allusion throughout the book to illustrate how uniquely different God has created humankind by using very definite patterns, yet enabling us to identify closely with other individuals. When we discover the ways in which we are alike and different, we will more readily accept ourselves and receive a new appreciation for others. We will learn the value and wholeness of each participant. Expect to have a lot of fun, to get some needed mental exercise, and to be challenged to make your world—our world—a happier place to live.

Open my eyes of understanding, Lord, that I may know who I am and appreciate who others are.

Notes

[1] Isabel Briggs Myers and Peter B. Myers, *Gifts Differing* (Palo Alto CA: Consulting Psychologists Press, 1980).

[2] Carl G. Jung is the originator of the theory of psychological type, and Isabel Briggs Myers and Katharine C. Briggs are authors of the Myers-Briggs Type Indicator.

[3] *Gifts Differing.*

Chapter 3

The Gift of Introversion

One who spares words is knowledgeable.
—Proverbs 17:27

When words are many, transgression is not lacking, but the prudent are restrained in speech.
—Proverbs 10:19

Introversion once implied that someone was inferior. Lucky or smart introverts would strive to be extroverted so that one day the line into normality would be crossed. The strange phenomenon is that even after introverts have entered the extroverted world, learned to assert themselves, become successful in business, gained great respect, and earned all kinds of academic degrees, they are still basically introverted in attitude and action. There is no permanent crossing of the line from one camp to the other, but only safe visitation rights or visas. Although introverts may envy the ease and optimism of extroverts and learn to develop it to some degree, when asked to choose how they prefer to be, they select their own more cautious introversion. Studies show that at least 25 percent of the population is naturally introverted.

> If a person prefers extroversion, his choice coincides with about 75 percent of the general population . . . Only 25 percent reported introversion as their preference, according to Myers."[1]

Introversion is a gift rather than a personality flaw or slight on God's part. No one is inferior, only misunderstood and unappreciated. God had good reasons for designing humans to be either extroverted or introverted, and we have as much choice in the matter as we had in choosing our sex or eye color.

As with other distinct characteristics, it's best to accept our particular gifts and use them to the advantage of ourselves and others. When we discover how introversion fits into God's plan, apologies cease. We can be like Martha, a soft-spoken and nonassertive young mother who, after she learned about her introverted social preference, leaned back on the sofa and signed, "You mean it's okay for me to be like I am?"

A confident and educated woman in her 80s who discovered that she was surely one of God's introverts, responded, "And all these years I've been confessing my sin in not being outgoing and not wanting to be around people a lot."

Many people mistakenly refer to anyone who is shy or quiet as an introvert. But shyness also bothers a few extroverts. Shyness is a learned attitude that can be overcome.

I've heard parents apologize for their child's lack of friendliness by saying, "She's strange or backward around people." Adults will even draw attention to a reserved child with, "Cat got your tongue?" For some reason, parents and teachers often believe it is inferior to be a person of few words. There is the story about a mother heard to protest loudly and defensively, "My daughter is not an introvert. She is a lovely girl!"[2]

Most people envy those who exude self-confidence and friendliness and have the ability to speak quickly and authoritatively. Western culture seems to sanction the outgoing, sociable, and gregarious temperament. The notion of anyone wanting or needing much solitude is viewed rather often as reflecting an unfriendly attitude. Solitary activities frequently are seen as ways to structure time until something better comes along, and this something better by definition involves interacting with people. Consequently, introverts are often the ugly ducklings in a society where the majority enjoy sociability.[3]

Surprisingly, many extroverts regard themselves as introverted, but they are confusing low self-esteem or lack of confidence with introversion. Loudness and boldness are not synonymous with extroversion. I've met some very noisy, assertive—even pushy—introverts as well as some relatively reserved and quiet extroverts.

A person does not decide to be quiet, reserved, noncommunicative, sober, cautious, fearful, or serious. Nor does a person develop into an introvert simply because of childhood experiences, neglect, or lack of social encounter. People are introverts because God, knowing that the world desperately needed a few, created them.

Technically, everyone is a unique blend of both extroversion and introversion, needing a dose of each to be balanced. But every person leans toward or prefers one tendency. Due to the extent of social exposure, people become either more strongly introverted or extroverted, or conversely, mildly introverted or extroverted. Some researchers label the latter as ambiverts, but I find that even borderline people definitely fall more comfortably into one camp more than the other.

Self-Evaluation

Characteristics of introverts are further explained below. Following each explanation is a self-evaluation question. If you can answer "yes," place a check in the box.

Mind Editing

Introverts think, then speak. Extroverts speak, then think—or think while they're speaking. They carry big erasers in their back pocket to wipe away what they didn't really mean or what didn't come out right. They open their mouths to change their feet. Without a doubt, the apostle Peter was an extrovert. For extroverts, not commenting is about as easy as not breathing. Introverts usually say what they mean and mean what they say. Don't knock either style; God designed both.

Introverts, it appears, are equipped with an extra apparatus that allows them to "hear with their brain" what they are about to say. So their responses are very nearly what they thought. However, extroverts' mental computers are not expansive enough to hear ahead of time their extensive words. The more extroverts try to work out exactly what they want to say, the more tangled their ideas become because they often don't know what they are thinking until they say it.

Introverts are often obliged to sort through extroverts' masses of words. Consequently, in the course of introverts' mental sifting and formulating of ideas, extroverts who think and speak fast often move on to another subject without giving any opportunity for conversation input. Many introverts have shared how disconcerting and discouraging this is. I hope this information will encourage extroverts to allow more response time for introverts.

❏ Do you think, then speak?

Silence

"Are you mad?" "Don't you like me?" "Are you not feeling well?" "Are you bored?" "Did I say or do something wrong?" Are these questions you hear often? If so, you may be an introvert. In an effort to explain the lack of words, smiles, and optimism, all these questions run through the minds of extroverts and usually on out of their mouths. Nothing separates or confuses like silence. "Anybody who's that quiet must have something to hide," one lady surmised. False.

One of my close friends said, "We introverts wait around to be asked for our opinion or ideas." When introverts finally speak, though, people listen. Some people—especially introverts—are reluctant to take verbal risks. This quietness and reluctance to reveal what they're thinking intimidates many extroverts. Introverts, on the other hand, are surprised and distressed about these negative impressions because they are actually shaking in their boots rather than feeling smug and confident.

❏ Are you usually silent?

Space

Introverts require a lot of privacy and few people, whereas extroverts need more people and less privacy. Introverts keep things to themselves and are withdrawn. Consequently, they are harder to get to know. Some people regard them as snobs, overly spiritual, dull, strange, even wise.

Mark came for counseling because every area of his life, except college, was giving him stress. His parents and siblings labeled him weird because he had little interest in dating. His father, slightly hard of hearing, badgered him to watch football on television. At the close of the day the pulsating household racket of appliances, conversation, clatter and bangs of dishes and pans, and blaring television amplified in his room, making it impossible for him to concentrate on his studies. To add to his problems, Mark worked in a raucous fast-food restaurant. His head ached, and his stomach churned. When he elected to study in the school library, his family felt shut out.

What a breakthrough when we discovered that Mark was a strong introvert and all these things—noise and lack of privacy—constantly violated his system. When his family became sensitive to his needs and dropped the household noise level, releasing him from noisy television and social expectations and giving him plenty of peace and privacy, his physical problems disappeared.

If being around people for long periods of time or being in a noisy crowd exhausts you, or if you leave parties early, you may be introverted. Introverts prefer to be by themselves and "come up for air" every now and then by talking to someone, whereas extroverts prefer to be with people most of the time and disappear occasionally into privacy for a "quick breather."

"I'd rather plow a field all day," a strong introvert declared, "than attend a family reunion for an hour." The draining effect of people seems to be the greatest distinction of this personality type. But without some people in their lives, introverts can become discouraged, obsessed with negativism, bored, and lacking in confidence.

☑ Do you require a lot of privacy?

Silence

Introverts do not normally instigate conversation but can join in warmly when encouraged, usually on a one-to-one basis. Introverts are also slow to talk about themselves, but extroverts can encourage them to open up and share.

Early morning conversation generally tires as well as annoys introverts, as John moaned, "When my wife's feet hit the floor in the morning, her mouth automatically spews out questions and comments. I don't want to converse first thing in the morning. I don't want to hear talk or decide anything. I just want to ease quietly into the day." One introverted woman told me she doesn't even put her glasses on until 10:00 AM, so she can avoid contact with the world.

Carlton, the husband I describe in *Appreciation—What Every Woman Still Needs* (Grand Rapids: Baker Book House, 1981), had for 16 years urged his wife to be up early, don an apron, cheerfully prepare breakfast, and be ready for dialogue. After discovering that by God's design Jan was an introvert and preferred to move quietly and privately into the day, he declared, "I've really been unfair to greet her as soon as I wake up with 'Good morning, dear, how about a good morning kiss and a big smile,' haven't I? From now on, I'll just let her sleep awhile. I don't mind fixing my own coffee if that's the way she really is." That's understanding!

As I counseled a strongly introverted husband and his outgoing bubbly wife, she would answer the questions directed to him before he got a chance. Finally, I requested that she give him time to respond. I'd ask the question, then wait and wait. I wondered if he heard me, if he understood the question, if he was reluctant to answer. Eventually, after long, uncomfortable minutes (probably just long seconds), he'd smile, nod slightly, and respond softly and briefly. He told me that dialogue was actually painful to him.

Introverts see nothing awkward about several people sitting in the same room saying nothing, whereas extroverts feel obligated—coerced, in fact—to greet, comment, pass the time of day with whomever enters the room, considering it nothing short of courtesy. Introverts prefer to wait until there is some significant, well-thought-out contribution to share. Being friendly and outgoing and full of casual conversation just does not characterize the average introvert.

❏ Do you prefer silence over talking?

Aversion to Noise

Strong introverts dislike noise. A husband of more than 20 years said, "My wife's loud yawns make me bristle." When asked, "Are you sensitive to noise?" a college student responded emphatically, "Noise just magnifies in my head until it nearly drives me crazy!" Immediately, an extrovert involved in the same session blurted out confidently, "I love noise!"

Extroverts merely tolerate a quiet house or car, whereas introverts yearn for noiselessness. A few introverts are ultrasensitive to only a few select noises such as crying children, machinery, or loud music.

One of the key problems in the marriage relationship of an extrovert and an introvert is the noise capacity. *Appreciation—What Every Woman Still Needs* describes Carlton's irritation with Jan who habitually left the kitchen cabinets ajar. He liked a tidy kitchen and reprimanded her for lacking orderliness. Her reason was a valid one, though: she hated the noise accompanying the cabinets' closure. "I can fix that," he declared. "I'll install magnetic closures to soften the bangs." A simple but super solution.

❏ Do you dislike noise?

Pessimism

By nature, introverts tend to be somewhat, if not greatly, pessimistic because they internalize everything. They are likely to see what won't work. Consequently, they often expect the worst to happen. "Keeps disappointment under control," one of them said. "I fear failure," a young executive admitted. "In fact," he continued, "I expect to fail." Despite this young man's fears, he has succeeded more than he has failed.

When knocked down, extroverts say, "I'll try again." Introverts say, "I'll never be knocked down again." Some introverts acknowledge that it worries them even when things go really well, because they fear that payday will soon come. Good fortune will end, and they'll have to pay the price.

"One negative thought, and I'm a goner," Heidi confided. "It's like alcoholism. One pessimistic or bad thought leads to another until I'm completely smashed. Even when I have bad thoughts about someone else, I condemn myself for thinking critical or abusive thoughts. Sometimes I wish I could just run away from myself." Heidi will never become an extrovert, but she can learn to spot lies she feeds herself.

Discovering the lies we tell about ourselves as well as those we tack onto others' comments is a beneficial exercise for both extroverts and introverts. William Backus and Marie Chapian address this self-talk problem in *Telling Yourself the Truth* (Bethany Fellowship: Minneapolis MN, 1980):

> As long as you're convinced that you can't change [your thoughts] you won't try. There have been many people who have believed they could never change. And yet, these same people have dug in and changed their misbeliefs in spite of themselves, and the result has been transformed lives.

Negativism is like using bleach full strength. It removes every trace of color and even eats holes right through the fabric. But when diluted, bleach is an excellent disinfectant and stain and odor remover. Just so, mild negativism is a blessing expressed in carefulness, caution, and discretion of speech —qualities that extroverts yearn to possess.

❏ Do you tend to be pessimistic?

Depression

Because introverts internalize their feelings and thoughts, they are more susceptible to depression. I've quizzed extroverts about depression, and most of them declare, "Oh yes, I get depressed." "How long does your depression last, longer than twenty minutes?" "About that long," most admit.

Extroverts sometimes wrongly label a down mood or upset as depression. But because extroverts are compelled to verbalize most of their thoughts, their lips act as springs that automatically bring people and conversation into their lives—the very therapy that dispels discouragement and disappointment. Thus, extroverts usually escape deep and long-lasting depression. I have met only a few who have actually battled deep depression.

It's easy to see why many introverts suffer with feelings of inadequacy since they find being assertive and verbally expressive so difficult. Nearly every introvert I've interviewed has expressed a strong desire to be more assertive because he or she feels inferior, being forced to compete in the noisy, rapid-paced, extroverted world.

Because pessimism and fear of failure plague introverts, acquiring self-confidence is slower. But once gained, self-appreciation and confidence is solid and sure. Even though every person needs a certain dose of compliments and approval, introverts are a bit embarrassed to receive positive appraisal. They dislike public recognition.

❏ Have you experienced real depression?

People Drain

The desire for privacy, sensitivity to noise, restrained conversation, and the tendency for pessimism and depression do not entirely determine one's social preference for introversion. The most distinctive characteristic is that draining effect of being around people, while being around people charges or tunes up an extrovert. People know the difference. This explains why introverted spouses are reluctant to have house guests and attend parties. When they do, they appear to be antisocial and are ready to leave early.

❏ Does being around people drain you?

If you answered yes to most of the preceding questions, you are no doubt an introvert. The world needs to learn how to understand and appreciate you.

Appreciating Introverts

God didn't goof when He created introverts. "So God created humankind in his image, in the image of God created he created them; male and female he created them; . . . God saw everything that he had made, and indeed, it was very good" (Gen 1:27, 31). Introverts are helped just by understanding this, as the following testimony indicates.

"After learning about introversion," Wanda declared, "I feel better. I thought that being quiet meant I had a poor personality and was somehow inferior to assertive people. Now that I realize I am quiet by nature, I have found self-esteem. I like myself better."

When extroverts are aware of the characteristics of introverts, they will wait longer for responses but will actively request opinions and conversation input. One introvert admitted, "I have plenty to say, but I'd rather someone ask me what I think than volunteer my opinion." Extroverts should also protect introverts from an overload of personal questions and small talk.

The deliberate attitude, thoroughness, and concentration abilities of introverts are commendable qualities for which many extroverts strive. Without the profound thoughts and ideas from introverts, extroverts would have less to discuss. So, rather than being a curse, introversion is a gift from God. Introverts often express themselves better on paper and choose writing over speaking. They make progress inside their heads. Unfortunately, many introverts who provide insight into the physical and intellectual world are not recognized, rewarded, or given credit for their ideas and expertise.

In Marriage

Velma describes one drawback that surfaces in her extrovert/introvert marriage. "Sam's disappointed that I'm so withdrawn, and I feel inadequate because I am ultra quiet. Sam keeps trying to get me to be more talkative and bold by drawing attention to me in a group. But I'm just not comfortable talking. People wear me out."

When extroverts are sensitive to their introverted spouses' reduced capacity for people, confusion, and noise, they will compromise by limiting exhausting social affairs. Sensitive extroverts can show their consideration and love by allowing introverted mates recouping time after a day of exhausting social exposure.

"When I come in from work," Marvin shared, "Joyce protects me from the children and telephone for 45 minutes while I either take a walk, read the paper, or lie down. I'm good for the rest of the evening then."

"Since we are both introverts," Chuck said, "and work with people all day, we rotate relief in the evening. I get my recouping time before dinner, then I'm totally in charge of the household for an hour after dinner while Clara has quiet time."

In the Family

Extroverted children seem to attract more positive attention from teachers and relatives, as well as from parents. When a child is quiet and withdrawn, the parent is likely to feel guilty and assumes the child is unhappy. Recently a troubled mother brought her 16-year-old daughter for counseling. "Try to find out what she's mad about," she begged. "I'm sure Cynthia has resentments because of our divorce. She never says anything. I wonder if she's on drugs," she continued. "I worry about her because she has very few friends and spends most of her time reading or listening to music or just doing nothing. She and her sister don't get along either."

In an hour I discovered that Cynthia was an introvert who found it difficult to get a word in edgewise at home. She had no resentments, particularly about the divorce, other than the altered finances and family time. She didn't have many friends because she didn't want many. She wasn't unhappy just because she didn't wear a wide grin all the time. Her sister's loud stereo and constant chatter violated her need for privacy and quiet after the day at school. This extroverted mother was using herself and her other daughter's outgoingness as the standard for normality.

It is not unusual for introverted children to be born into extroverted homes and vice versa. In my childhood family of six children, only my older sister is introverted. However, no one would guess it by the way she's learned to adjust as a matter of survival in a crowd of extroverts. I do remember, though, how she'd disappear into her room and bury herself in a book. We thought she was just being lazy, when actually she was grabbing private time after being at school all day. Parents need to be sensitive to their children's requirement for space and time to recoup.

When children become aware that one or both parents is introverted, sensitive to noise, and easily tired by conversation, they, too, will become less demanding and more understanding. Introverted mothers, often overly conscientious, can live in violation of their temperament only so long before they revolt with illness or complete discouragement and frustration. Understanding could ease homes of much avoidable tension, irritability, and anger. I believe much child abuse is rooted in adults' low tolerance for noise and confusion.

How difficult it must have been for my introverted mother to rear six noisy, rambunctious children almost alone. How she managed to avoid child abuse is beyond me. I'm confident her strong faith and dependence on God gave her extra endurance. I can understand and accept now that fulfilling my demand for talking attention was an emotional overload for her.

At School

Introverted children tend to be shy, quiet, and less intrusive than extroverted children. Introverted children are apt to be slower in responsiveness, musing over an idea or object, seeming to absorb its qualities before communicating a reaction. Thus, at times they may seem less intellectually capable than they actually are. Introverted children are inclined to develop their habits more slowly than do extroverted children. Introverts reserve from "public view" those aspects of their temperament that are in process of development, presenting to the "public" only those qualities that are already developed. Only too often introverted children are judged as "stubborn" by well-meaning adults, because they insist on holding back their responses until they have rehearsed internally.[4] Asking an introverted child to act like an extrovert damages the child, and most often that is the change we want to make.

Unfortunately, schools are not geared for introverts. How often teachers say, "Now students, half of your grade is determined by class participation."

Extroverts will volunteer ideas before they even have a full idea, leaving introverts intimidated and lagging behind. A study indicates that the average public school teacher waits about five seconds for responses to questions. When counseled regarding this, a group of teachers lengthened their wait to 10 seconds—still not fair for introverts.

"Teachers appreciate a shy kid so they can ignore him or her," an introverted mother surmised. "I don't think my daughter's teacher even knows she exists. She's being ignored because she's quiet."

Another type of mistreatment occurs regularly and innocently at the hands of extroverted teachers.

Estelle, a middle-aged woman struggling for self-esteem, recalled a traumatic violation of her introversion when she was a schoolgirl. "The teacher thought a story I wrote was very good and encouraged me to read it before the class. I was frightened into a headache and requested to go to the nurse. Consequently, I received a bad grade on an 'A' paper simply because I was afraid to read aloud."

Teachers and parents who try to teach children that their natural, retiring, introverted ways are wrong are setting in motion attitudes and impressions that those children will have to work to overcome the rest of their lives.

At Work

Introverted employees often assume that the boss is displeased and the office crew doesn't enjoy having them around, even though their evaluations are positive. They continually find fault with their critical thoughts and fear that someone could do a better job. This internalizes their self-hate, forming a slush fund that putrefies. Many introverts eventually turn to antidepressants or other drugs to relieve their tension rather than get to the root of their problem, which is low self-esteem resulting from ignorance about God's special design of introversion. Not liking the way you are is not normal and is not God's desire. Psalm 18:32-36 encourages introverts:

> The God who girded me with strength, and made my way safe. He made my feet like the feet of a deer, and set me secure on the heights. He trains my hands for war, so that my arms can bend a bow of bronze. You have given me the shield of your salvation, and your right hand has supported me; your help has made me great. You gave me a wide place for my steps under me, and my feet did not slip.

Many introverts are overlooked for promotion because they are content to wait to be noticed. Some introverts criticize extroverts for using introverts to politicize their jobs. But people who respond quickly and talk confidently grab the boss's attention and admiration.

At Church

Perhaps because introverts recognize their need for encouragement and help, they seem to be more spiritually minded and fill our churches. However, they are slower to make public decisions about trusting Christ, preferring to do it privately.

"I thought the goal of spiritual maturity was to be like those people I admire who can talk to anyone and seem to have answers for all life's questions," Phyllis said. "Now I know the goal is to be satisfied that God designed me to prefer one person at a time."

Many introverts really are asking and expecting God to make assertive, expressive, confident people out of them and take away their problems in answer to their prayers. God's way may be to give them endurance to work their way through introverted traits that will in the process increase their assertiveness, expression, and confidence and raise their self-esteem. Once we yank out the irrationalities and lies from our thoughts and replace them with the truth, we can lead satisfying, rich, and fulfilling emotional lives.

First Corinthians 10:13 promises that God will not give us more than we can bear. "Oh, yeah?" most problem-plagued people challenge. "Well, I've had more than I can bear!" The last part of that verse offers the relief: "He will also provide the way out so that you may be able to endure it." Our way out is a friend, a counselor, a church fellowship, the Scriptures, and prayer.

"I'm afraid if I start a Christian life, I can't continue it," Mary said. Introverts are often so negative and fearful anyway, they regard conviction of sin as something negative rather than a warm reminder by the Holy Spirit when actions and thoughts are wrong.

Much of corporate worship violates introverts—loud music, public praying, discussion, testimony, and the like.

Conclusion

If you are an introvert, I hope you now appreciate your gift more. Smile a little more if you don't feel like talking to let the extroverts know you're not mad. And if you are an extrovert, I trust you will be more sensitive to the quieter segment of our society and give them a chance to talk and the respect and recognition they deserve.

One of the benefits of being introverted is that when someone violates their conscience or personality, introverts know where to draw the line.

Introverts are easy to spot on our bicycle trip because they are generally riding alone or with just one or two others.

Lord, enable me to be warm and at least smile at others, even if I don't feel like talking. Help me not to put myself down for getting weary of people. Grant me optimism and enthusiasm about your work. Give me courage to speak up when extroverts are wording—conversing— roughshod over me.

Notes

[1] Keirsey and Marilyn Bates, *Please Understand Me* (Del Mar CA: Prometheus Nemesis Books, 1978) 16.

[2] Ibid.

[3] Ibid.

[4] Ibid.

Chapter 4

The Ease and Art of Extroversion

From the fruit of the mouth one is filled with good things, and manual labor has its reward.

—Proverbs 12:14

"An encourager"
"A nonstop talker"
"All mouth and no brain"
"A person who can take over"
"An outgoing and friendly person"
"Someone who has nerves of steel"

The question, "What is an extrovert?" brings interesting answers. To some people, being extroverted is the same as being aggressive, brash, nervy, brazen-faced, offensive, loud, and defiant. Other people view extroverts as energetic, confident, enthusiastic, dynamic, tireless, tough-skinned, and suave.

"I hate being insecure," complained an introvert. "I'd give anything to be optimistic and able to talk easily, like my extroverted sister."

"I wish I were not so bold," an extrovert piped up. "Sometimes I think I have three tongues!"

What extroverts seem to do effortlessly, introverts have to work toward. However, most extroverts assume that the ease and confidence with which they speak and act is natural to anyone who will work at it a little. Consequently, they often take credit for developing their own personalities when, in essence, they are merely functioning the way their Creator fashioned them.

A few extroverts even smugly assume that their natural optimism and confidence are results of their own faith and therefore quite possible for anyone. This supposition intimidates many introverts, who at times feel spiritually inferior to confident, outspoken, and brightly optimistic extroverts.

"I wish I had your courage and faith," an introvert will say with envy. "Quit worrying about yourself, and you can have it!" comes the extrovert's glib reply. Dependence on the Lord and growth in faith are uniquely different for introverts and extroverts. Understanding both extremes promises appropriate appreciation.

Extroversion means a preference for sociability over solitude, for external over internal. And for 75 percent of society, needing people outweighs the need for privacy. Thus, the more the merrier is the philosophy of the majority who hunger for conversation, have positive attitudes, and are assertive. Like introverts, however, extroverts appear in varying strengths, though still sharing a few definite distinctives.

Extroverts can tolerate confusion and noise; some seem to thrive on it. Their personal confidence baffles as well as impresses the more cautious introverted segment of society. Usually extroverts give the impression of being secure, unafraid, and able to handle most situations.

Strange as it may seem, many people with this personality type struggle relentlessly with shyness and low self-esteem, quite unable to utilize their gift of extroversion. Likewise, some introverts have learned the art of conversation so well that they appear quite outgoing. This means that not all quiet or shy people are necessarily introverted, or that all talkative, assertive, confident people are extroverted.

Some introverts are fluent talkers because an inborn drive to help and serve people and to succeed forces them to be outgoing and loquacious at times. Therefore, distinguishing introverts from extroverts is not always easy.

Knowing that one is an extrovert by God's design relaxes a person to be what he or she really is, quiets the tendency to degrade oneself for needing people and noise, and assures him or her that it's normal and okay to be talkative. This knowledge also pinpoints one's areas of greatest potential and reveals the strong traits that could be modified at times in the interest of introverts' capacities and preferences.

Self-Evaluation

Characteristics of extroverts are further explained below. Following each explanation is a self-evaluation question. If you can answer "yes," place a check in the box.

Earshot Editing

Extroverts are prone to speak, then think; or they think while they are in the process of speaking. Extroverts have to talk! "I don't know what I'm thinking until I say it," Martha admitted. "I just hate that I often have to qualify what I have said." "I can't think unless I speak," John stated. "If I explain something to you, then I can understand it myself."

Extroverts speak out quickly and often don't always say exactly what they mean. Tripping over the tongue is a common malady—remember, the big erasers in their back pockets are used daily. Extroverts have to decide after they hear what they say or get the reaction of their hearers whether or not what they just said was what they meant. They may not even wait until a question is completed before they begin to answer. Often comments or answers to questions, though not necessarily complete mentally, formulate only as extroverts speak.

But God created this type of mind to have to hear with their ears what they are thinking. That's why extroverts may show surprise—pleasure or displeasure—at an idea or comment that tumbled, or bumbled, out of their mouths. Introverts cringe at the thought of earshot editing in public.

❏ Do you generally speak before or while you think?

Motor Mouth

Extroverts cannot function without human sounding boards. They talk about themselves and their problems easily. This is not a flaw of character or an insecurity; extroverted minds just happen to function opposite to introverted minds. Many of extroverts' problems are solved as they are in the process of describing them.

Wanda began talking as soon as she entered the counseling room. The only words I uttered were "Uh, huh," "I see," "Hmmm," "That's interesting." Yet, after our hour, she rose quickly, hugged me, and said, "You've been more help to me than anyone I've ever counseled with. I think you're wonderful!"

Usually extroverts have no difficulty speaking out or being heard. In classes they are generally the first to raise their hands. If they make a verbal mistake, they easily shrug it off with, "That didn't come out right," or "Did I say that?"

Extroverts miss very few opportunities for conversation input. In fact, they are likely to put words in other people's mouths or finish another's sentence. They are prone to rattle on and on. As one extrovert confessed, "I apologize for talking your ear off." Such personalities have a tendency to overexplain their position, actions, and intentions.

Extroverts are often uncomfortable with conversation lulls. "I figure if there's a lull," one young woman declared, "someone has to fill it. If no one talks, there's tension. I talk to keep tension under control," she defended.

Although introverts will do public speaking when circumstances demand, extroverts delight in and look for opportunities to speak or lead. "He just likes to hear his own voice" is the appraisal one often hears.

❑ Does talking a lot and about yourself come easy for you?

Need for People

Extroverts need a lot of people and just a little bit of privacy. They prefer to work with people in jobs where conversation is not only possible but also necessary. Being alone for long periods usually distresses them. In fact, some have need of conversation the greater part of the day.

"My day is just laced together with conversation," Julie said. "I go crazy in a quiet house. If I can't have people, I turn the radio or TV on for company. I'd die without a telephone."

Needing people is not a weakness, but a gift. Whereas introverts function better in a one-on-one situation, extroverts prefer a crowd.

❑ Do you need a lot of people?

Love of Noise

Most extroverts have a high tolerance for noise, even though they may not say they love it. "As soon as Rob gets in the car, the radio or tape player goes on," Angie griped. "I feel like taking a hammer to it sometimes!" "She accuses me of trying to drown out my problems, including her," Ed defended, "but that's not so. I'm just more comfortable with a background of noise. Actually, noise helps me think better."

❑ Do you enjoy noise?

Fast and Full Pace

Most extroverts seem to think fast, talk fast, and decide fast. They are also quick to volunteer and want to get moving right away. Because their minds are often cluttered with people-involvements, they may not be as thorough as introverts who have the ability to concentrate on one thing at a time.

"My mouth gets me into more trouble," Donna analyzed. "I never have the time to do all the things for which I volunteer. If I could disconnect my tongue," she mused, "I'd have some time for myself."

❑ Do you prefer a fast/full pace?

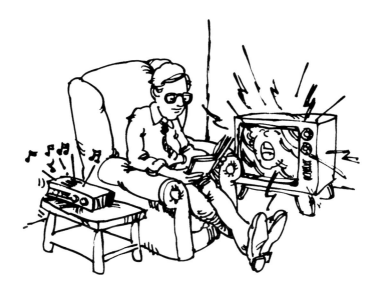

Optimistic

Extroverts are more likely to see positive aspects in a situation and look on the bright side of things. Extroverts do not expect to fail. In fact, they protect themselves by not trying the things they feel sure they cannot do, rather than risk the embarrassment of failure. "We'll try it. If it doesn't work, we'll try something else."

Extroverts seem to be lighthearted and to laugh easily, at themselves especially. Generally they are not plagued with moodiness, and they will intentionally brighten up a dreary day with enthusiastic jesting or endeavor to get a party spirit rolling. For example, they may bring treats to the office to encourage total participation.

Long-term depression is seldom found in extroverts. Introverted spouses ask: "Aren't you ever serious?" "Doesn't anything ever bother you?" Extroverts may become discouraged and disappointed for a time, but their self-confidence and optimism, like a hydraulic jack, steadily raises them.

❑ Are you fairly optimistic and confident?

By now you should know whether or not you are extroverted, and to what degree. Remember, the most distinctive trait of an extrovert is that being around people charges your battery rather than drains it. If you are an extrovert, the introverted world needs to learn how to understand and appreciate you.

Appreciating Extroverts

For God to design the large majority of people to be extroverted indicates that the world evidently needs what such folks contribute. While most introverts think they would give their eyeteeth to be extroverted, there are a few drawbacks that bug most extroverts at some time. Introverts should wipe their brows in relief that they do not have to contend with such problems. For example, it is easier for an introvert to imitate an extrovert rather than vice versa.

"I've tried to be quiet for an entire hour," Phil said, "and everyone around thinks I'm sick, mad, or troubled."

Society sometimes allows introverts to be quiet for hours at a time, but extroverts cannot get away with the same silence, as I proved with a little experiment one time. Six adult family members, all but one extroverted, were traveling together, and for a brief time I made no comment and started no conversation. Gradually, as the others became aware of my quietness, they also became uncomfortably quiet. Then I caught bewildered glances followed by concern. "You okay, Mom?" "Yes, I'm fine." Long silence. No one talked. "Are you feeling all right, Honey?" Jim asked. "Fine." "I thought maybe you wanted to stop." I resumed my normal talkativeness and only later revealed what I had intentionally done. "I thought you were mad," our daughter said. "I thought maybe you and Dad had fallen out over something, even though I heard nothing."

Extroverts have a hard time handling lack of conversation. Their minds go cavorting all over the place. Someone has suggested that quiet people are under more control, which is somewhat true. When someone is an extrovert, it seems, they are obliged to converse.

What You Hear Is What You Get

Extroverts more easily share their feelings. They tell it all as soon as anyone will listen. Sharing intimate experiences is not difficult for them. Introverts are even uncomfortable hearing personal data. Often extroverts suffer rejection because after they've spilled everything, their opposite types retain their reserve. Thus, embarrassed and disappointed, extroverts leave themselves wide open for criticism, betrayal, and loss of respect.

Although extroverts may appear thick-skinned, they do suffer from verbal abuse and from not being taken seriously. Because they express positive evaluation and appreciation quickly, profusely, and often, their excessive pronouncements are often barely acknowledged. Even though deaf-ear experiences can teach wordy people to modify and edit their verbal contributions, extroverts are still sensitive to overt rejection, disrespect, and discourtesy.

Extroverts need to know how they are heard. Fortunate are those who have a friend that will patiently and kindly critique their conversations by making a list of sarcasms, exaggerations, and violations. Most extroverts appreciate a caring friend's constructive criticism.

In Marriage

Marriage to an extroverted person presents opportunities for adjustment on the part of the less outgoing spouse.

"Now that I understand my spouse's need for morning cheers, I'll start the day with, 'How's my little extrovert this morning?' then go off alone," Ron grinned sheepishly.

When riding together, a compromise on volume as well as frequency of radio or stereo, respecting both needs, will ease tension. Appreciating and adopting the outgoing spouse's bright temperament will lighten many gloomy days and soften unpleasant responsibilities.

Extroverts' resilience in defeat can inspire the entire family, giving children or spouse encouragement to try again or helping them not to worry about a project that flopped. "If at first you don't succeed, try, try again" must certainly have been spoken by an extrovert.

"Rob's friendliness attracted me," Sharon said. "When I was with him, I felt safe because I didn't have to worry about talking. He drew me out and shared his friends with me. I know I gained a lot of personal confidence, but now I resent that he wants to have other people around all the time. I'm not enough. I feel totally inadequate. But at the same time, I get sick of hearing his voice, and I'm glad someone else is there to listen. Isn't it strange that the things that attracted me to Rob in the first place seem to be the traits that bug me most now?"

Extroverts will inevitably attract and invite people to their homes. Although this may frighten an introverted spouse, this love for people will open many interesting doors and add new dimensions to the marriage and family relationship. In fact, extroverts may need to be cautioned about how often and how many people to entertain. But refusal or criticism of socializing robs extroverts of an important source of self-esteem that comes from friendships and verbal feedback, which, incidentally, introverts need as well. Many conversation-hungry spouses end up at the bar or local hangout.

In the Family

"Janie is about to get me down," Bonnie admitted. "She's very bold, for one thing. She brings not one friend home from school, but would you believe five or six? She's constantly surrounded by people. When she's not with her friends, she's on the telephone, which poses another problem. She's asked for her own line, but I think she needs some time to rest her tongue and mind as well as to be with the family. She's never quiet a minute. She just exhausts me!"

From the time they are quite young, extroverted children draw others around them. Their enthusiasm, smiles, and courage benefit them in the classroom and in hospitals because teachers and nurses respond with the special attention they demand. Medical journals agree that extra eye contact and dialogue enable outgoing children to make faster progress.

Extroverted children crave extensive dialogue time with parents. If the mother is introverted, as mine was, extra understanding and appreciation will be needed from both parties. Children can learn to accept the fact that a parent requires more quiet time.

Awarding children personal time to talk—perhaps after school when they are full to the brim—not only will be satisfying, but also will help them become fully acquainted with themselves (remember, extroverts don't know what they think until they talk) and will build the rapport and understanding necessary for good family communication.

Extroverted children can understand that morning is not the time for animated conversation with their introverted parents, so long as the children are confident that their parents are not just putting off listening altogether. To shut up an extroverted child for the sake of one's own peace and quiet is to shut the child out and put a lid on self-esteem.

In desperation, extroverted children of introverted parents may turn to other adults or peers to share their dreams, opinions, and fears. In such a child-parent relationship, developing many confidences is the benefit, but losing close parental time and approval is the drawback. A balance of the two is a worthy goal.

At School

School is designed primarily for extroverts, because teachers favor their confident, quick thinking and speaking abilities. Giving oral book reports, reciting poems and multiplication tables, and reading aloud are easier for those who have a natural public poise.

School life can stifle extroverts, however, when it is all writing with no verbal expression, no whispering, and limited time for socializing (staying in for recess was the worst punishment for me). Rarely do extroverted children get good marks in conduct if whispering, talking, and moving about are not permitted. Enforced silence is a challenge.

School was my favorite arena because teachers acknowledged and appreciated my confidence and ability to speak and lead. However, I received "B's" in conduct, no matter how hard I tried.

At Work

As long as extroverts can have verbal contact with others, they can enjoy their employment, though many are misplaced and wasted in lone-ranger jobs. However, such employees, because of their love for "batting the breeze," are likely to waste their employer's time.

"Because I see no one all day," Barry, a strong extrovert, declared, "I'm bored to death with my warehouse job. I don't even have a telephone to answer. Filling written orders and checking silent files all day long drives me crazy. When I get home to my introverted wife, I drive her up the wall because I talk her ear off. While I am antsy to go some place and see people or attend a party, she prefers to stay home and enjoy some solitude after spending her day in a busy office. By 5 PM she's tired of people." Uncongenial employment like this will surely produce an ulcer or cause a mental explosion of some kind.

"I'd rather be selling peanuts on the square," Barry sighed. If he doesn't adjust his employment, not only his health will be in jeopardy, but also his marriage. Living in violation of God's design for us will provoke an eruption after a while.

At Church

Expressing faith seems to come more easily for extroverts because optimism and personal confidence come naturally, and transferring their trust from themselves to God doesn't seem like such a big step. But they have to be careful not to run ahead of God.

Because religious training emphasizes lay leadership, church situations provide a comfortable arena for extroverts to practice their fearless leading and sharing via informal classroom settings.

Open testimony time, which many church fellowships include, particularly appeals to extroverts who think quickly and are unafraid of extemporaneous speaking. Such outgoing ones need to be careful not to hog the show, however, and to trim their verbal offerings.

Small group Bible studies such as Sunday school where class participation is encouraged may be composed largely of extroverts, because they welcome a chance to speak and discuss. Unless extroverts say it out loud, they're not really sure what they believe. However, their extensive speaking often discourages others who prefer to hear what the teacher has to say. Introverts may stay away or seek lecture situations for fear someone will call on them to read or talk.

Extroverts are quicker to volunteer for committee work because they are not afraid of meeting new people. They may actively promote changes, but if church leaders are not careful, they may discover that church programs have become geared to extroverts' preferences for large gatherings where everyone is expected to speak, lead, or teach. Extroverts enjoy greeting people and making others feel welcome. Worship services that include a get-acquainted time appeal to extroverts, but may frighten others.

Paul Tournier says in *The Strong and the Weak* that whereas introverts depend on God to increase their self-confidence, extroverts depend on God to modify their self-confidence. Extroverts generally prefer spoken prayers because they need to hear what they are praying so they can control or direct their thoughts. A good prayer for extroverts is: "Lord, help me to depend on your wisdom and to wait longer than I want to before I speak. Help me to be sensitive to those quieter than I. Teach me to be a good listener."

Conclusion

Our extroverted bike riders group together to guarantee plenty of joking interchanges, singing, and laughing most of the way. One's ears can spot them.

Set a guard over my mouth, O Lord. Keep watch over the door of my lips. Help me to be more sensitive to introverts.

Chapter 5

Facts and Figures Fans

Let the favor of the Lord our God be upon us, and prosper for
us the work of our hands—O prosper the work of our hands!
—Psalms 90:17

Two simple processes involve us daily—gathering information and deciding what to do with it.

- Feel a draft—shut the door.
- Taste the soup—add salt.
- Hear the alarm—crawl out of bed.
- Survey the yard—start the lawnmower.
- Scan the want ads—buy a car.
- Sense hurt feelings—apply emotional hospitality.
- Study a book—take a test.
- Learn company is coming—clear your schedule.
- Check the calendar—winterize your automobile.
- Plan a night out—save some money.

One goal in everyone's life is to make good, solid decisions. However, wise decisions depend on quality fact-gathering. Collecting the data before taking action is the wisest method. Naturally, this order improves with maturity. Haven't we all been chided: "Why don't you think before you act?" "Use your head for something besides your hat!"

Information can be gathered in two ways, and decisions can be made by two methods. Everyone gathers or perceives in both ways at times and employs both methods for deciding or acting, depending on the situation. By God's design, however, each individual relies on one of these ways of information-gathering and especially trusts one particular method of decision making.

We can use our gifts for doing evil and for selfish pursuits or for right living and satisfying relationships. Although each person has a preferred way of gathering information—by sensing or by intuition—it is by consulting and depending on God's wisdom that we learn to exercise our best potential.

Since we use all these processes interchangeably throughout the day, picking out one's individual preferences may require some reflection. Why is knowing our preferences important? According to the Myers psychologist team,

> The kind of perception and the kind of judgment people naturally prefer determines the direction in which they can develop most fully and effectively and with most personal satisfaction. When people use their two best-liked processes in a purposeful effort to do something well, their skill with those processes increases.[1]

Discovering my inborn preference influenced a drastic change from full-time teaching to full-time counseling. I was happy as a teacher, but I've never been more fulfilled than I am now. We need to discover how God made us, and then live that way.

Getting acquainted with yourself—finding out how God gifted you—is the finest favor you can do for yourself. When you understand your pattern, you can then have the proper appreciation for what you are equipped to do and avoid putting yourself down for not matching another's accomplishments.

With this personal release from competition comes a natural appreciation for others who cannot accomplish what you find so easy to do. When families and teachers and employers understand one another's areas of expertise and responsibilities, our world becomes a saner and more peaceful place.

Sensing—Alive to the Physical World

The most popular way of gathering information is through one's five senses. According to Keirsey and Bates, "75 percent of the general population reports a preference for sensation, while 25 percent indicates a preference for intuition."[2]

Sensing-preference people are alive to the physical world. They tend to believe what they see, hear, taste, touch, and smell. Because they rely on their senses to supply the majority of their information, they are closer to the visible world.

Characteristics of sensing-preference people are explained below. Following each explanation is a self-evaluation question. Check the areas that most closely describe you, and your God-designed preferences will surface. Developing your preferred processes will help you to work toward and realize your potential, even if you are past 40.

Visual Perception

When visual-sensing people walk or ride, they automatically see birds, rocks, potholes, abandoned cars, cracks in the sidewalk, and new paint jobs on houses. They read newspapers thoroughly, picking up tiny bits of news. Because they are super observant of the world around them, giving detailed descriptions of people and events is their special talent.

A visually observant friend recently amazed me when she said she could remember what I had worn to church for the last four Sundays. "That's better than what I can dredge up," I admitted. "From now on to avoid outfit reruns, I'll call you before I needlessly rack my brain." Intuitive people are usually less observant.

Because visual-sensing people are especially sensitive to color, texture, and lines, they enjoy working with clothing, materials, interior decorations, and the like. Their homes are usually well kept, attractive, comfortable, and convenient. Attractive, stylish, but practical, clothing will fill their closets.

Visual sensing people are conscientious about keeping their homes dusted, walks and porches swept, cars washed, shoes shined, nails polished, lawns mowed, gardens weeded, leaves raked, and windows shining.

❏ Are you visually sensitive?

Audible Perception

Audio-sensing people are finely tuned to faraway thunder, sirens, creature noises, house creakings, and the latest gossip. Many enjoy listening to and playing music. Television, radio, and movies generally attract these people.

Sensing people often use radio scanners to pick up facts that keep them apprised of all the neighborhood happenings. As Jim and I visited with such a man, he'd tilt his head, raise his hand, and say, "Hold it!" until he could catch the dispatcher's report. In fact, he had two scanners going all day long. Some buffs even carry portable sets. They want to know what's going on.

Sensing people are generally patient listeners. They rarely forget facts they hear or the order in which they heard them. Watching or playing sports seems to have a greater pull on sensing persons than on intuitives. Their love for repeated actions, combined with expertise in facts and figures, enables them to recall football plays from years past, giving minute details—downs, yardages, who tackled whom, how many minutes were left on the clock. Such talent amazes those who do not have the interest or ability.

❏ Are you audibly super alert?

Touch Perception

Doing something with their hands is a preference of touch-sensing people, whether it be wood or metal working, sewing, cooking, playing an instrument, weaving, mechanical tinkering, molding, hairdressing, photography, painting, planting, scrubbing, or canning. They enjoy mending and building, and do not mind repeating the same actions. Touch-perceptive people are attracted to delicate, tedious jobs such as surgery, sculpting, watch making and repair, nursing, accounting, and electronics.

"As long as my hands are busy, I'm not bored," said a sensing person. "But let my hands be idle, and I can't control my thoughts." Intuitives are just the opposite. If their minds are not involved, even if their hands are, they lose their inner balance.

Intuitives can learn to do intricate manipulations but are often bored after awhile, finding that repeating a design or an action is almost unbearable. I admire and appreciate those who enjoy or tolerate factory work or spend the majority of their lifetime performing physical jobs.

I read of a lady who for 21 years stacked crackers on a conveyor belt all day long, rarely missing the exact number of crackers to be wrapped. She loved her job. Never tired of it. Amazing! And there are people who patiently operate machines hour after hour, year after year.

❏ Do you enjoy working with your hands?

Smell and Taste Perception

Sensing people who are especially reactive to smells and tastes are often good cooks and bakers and enjoy "setting a good table." Their meals tend to be practical and nutritious as well as attractive, and sharing their culinary treats with friends is a special delight. Preparing the same meals over and over doesn't seem to bore them. Generally they stick with the basics and follow recipes to the letter instead of experimenting. They even have a recipe for tea.

Dining out can also be a favorite pastime for these people. They usually know the best restaurants for the best price, and when they find a good place to eat, they are likely to go there often, whereas intuitives find the same atmosphere and menus boring. They may waste time and money, however, looking for variety.

❏ Are you sensitive to smell and taste?

Sticklers for Facts

Although everyone is forced to use their senses because physical survival depends on it, those who prefer the sensing process are marked by their definite expertise in discovering and remembering facts. They respect facts, remember facts, collect stacks of facts, and want them accurate. "When my wife comes home from shopping for a new dress," Phil said, "I don't want her to say it cost somewhere around $25. I want to know exactly how much."

Fact-lovers usually know how much money they have in their pockets. Sometimes intuitives cannot even find their money, let alone remember how much they have. Rarely do sensing persons forget a price, an experience, details of an argument, or where they put something. Their stories teem with names, places, times, etc., whereas intuitives hit the high points—skim. They just want to know who won.

We used to stop our eldest son in the middle of a detailed account of a softball game to ask, "Did you sneeze on third base?" Now that we know he is fact-loving by preference, we understand why trivia is so important to him. He enjoys telling and retelling the same stories in the same way without interruption.

Sensing people are more interested in what happened than in what might happen. This makes them especially interested in things like history, tradition, and family reunions. Because they respect facts so much, their decisions are not likely to be impulsive. "I like to sleep on a matter," a sensing husband said. "Yeah, he sleeps on it for weeks," quipped his intuitive wife.

"My wife shopped all day for a lamp," Marvin shared. "Although she found exactly what she wanted at the very first store, she continued to look. After hours of comparing and figuring, sure enough," he chuckled, "she trekked right back to store number one and purchased the first lamp she admired." She was a sensing person.

Sensing people enjoy teaching straight facts. Because they are comfortable with repetition, teaching children particularly draws them. Often their questions are: Who's going? How much money do I need?

Faith in facts is usually further emphasized by ease in working with practical math. Money matters are more fun than frustrating (perhaps until it comes to balancing a tight personal budget). Spending all day in accounting or keeping numerical details, filling in little blanks, requires the diligence and patience of a fact-sensing person.

❏ Do you enjoy gathering facts and working with figures?

Conservers

Great conservers generally are sensing people. They know how much money they have in their wallets and in their checking accounts. They dislike wasting money, time, or possessions, and as a rule, are reluctant to take great monetary risks.

Conservers usually take good care of their automobiles, bicycles, and appliances. Often they are the shade-tree mechanics as well as career mechanics. They would rather mend an item than buy a new one. But it's easy for them to repair things because they possess mechanical ability. Often they become very attached to things they have repaired or attempted to repair. If you find fault with the way it sounds or performs, sensing people are prone to take it personally.

Home solar systems, economy cars, fluorescent lighting, microwaves, anything that saves energy, time, or money attracts them. You'll find many sensing types at yard sales. Buying a good tool or garment for a dollar, even when they don't need it, is a great satisfaction. Sensing people tend to hoard things; their garages bulge with pieces of wire, nails, screws, and old parts. Junkyards seem to hold special fascination for this type.

❏ Are you economical and careful to conserve resources?

Experience-Decisions

Sensing people base their decisions primarily on facts at hand and past experiences. The more experiences they have had, the wiser their judgment becomes—or the more reluctant they are to attempt something that has already been tried and found wanting.

This is where common sense enters. Generally, sensing people learn from their mistakes. If they bog down in a muddy road, they avoid getting stuck a second time. Experience is reliable. "If it worked well once, why change it?" they'll say. "Don't fix it if it isn't broken," a sensing man said. Sensing people usually wait to change or improve something until they bump into a problem with the old design. "We've always done it this way," or "We stick with tradition," is descriptive.

Sensing types want solutions to be workable. They are hard workers and depend on perspiration and effort. They have difficulty understanding those who avoid or dislike manual labor. Sensing people are realists; today interests them more than tomorrow. For this reason, many enjoy country-western, slice-of-life song lyrics. Because they like experience, they enjoy hearing family stories again and again, and love familiar tunes. "Don't spoil my favorite hymns by arranging them so that tantalizing tidbits of the tune are heard only now and then," one of my older sensing friends exclaimed.

❏ Do you rely on past experiences in decision making?

Sensing Conversation

Because sensing people prefer facts, figures, and experiences, when these sources are depleted, they soon fall into silence. So, they are pretty dependent on having experiences in common with someone before they can enjoy and maintain conversation. Although extroverted sensing people are the most talkative, they need facts in common to fuel dialogue.

An introverted sensing farmer friend of mine is quiet as a mouse until someone mentions tractors. Then his face brightens, his eyes light up, and his voice is finally heard. He knows a lot about tractors, and he doesn't mind sharing his knowledge.

An extroverted sensing lady, who wanted to converse with male co-workers, gathered football facts so she would have something to say. When the fellows discussed a subject in which she was not knowledgeable, she would do research so she could join in their chatter. An intuitive would prefer to learn unknown facts by asking questions. They may not know all the facts, but they never run out of questions.

Complex, technical, theoretical, theological, or philosophical discussions bore most sensing people quickly. They prefer to talk about what has actually happened or how something works. They never tire of reminiscing, whereas intuitives prefer new-ideas conversation, asking "Why?" and "How come?"

❏ Do you respond best in a conversation that involves having facts in common?

Product People

Sensing people especially enjoy doing things with their hands. They are product people who receive much of their confidence and self-esteem from visible accomplishments. Some intuitives make things with their hands, but their most natural achievements are linked to design, ideas, and problem-solving.

Because sensing people have the ability to see how things physically fit together and work, they enjoy adjusting, correcting, repairing, or maintaining equipment and materials. Lucky is the intuitive who has a sensing mate. Jim keeps everything running efficiently and smoothly at our house. He can figure out almost any mechanical problem, whereas I give up easily.

I have been Jim's secretary for as long as we've been married and have done my best to produce error-free stencils and bulletins. No matter how hard I have tried, though, he usually finds something wrong, which he proceeds to correct with great relish. Making the mistake is bad enough for me, but having someone insist on correcting it makes it doubly intolerable.

However, when I learned that he really wasn't being overly picky, but that he actually enjoyed mending, correcting, and straightening, I thought, "Why fight it? If he enjoys it, why deprive him?" (Of course, computers have eliminated this struggle.)

Sensing people take great pride in decorating and cleaning houses, manicuring lawns, and maintaining picturesque vegetable gardens. They want their work to meet the standards and to adequately fulfill the need. This is why many sensing people enjoy selling tangibles.

I'll never forget observing a lady sitting alone embroidering a huge bedspread in a lounge area of a motel where I attended a meeting. She was still there at lunchtime. I admired her work and inquired, "How long will it take you to finish?" "Oh, about a month working pretty steadily." "Don't you ever tire of doing this?" "Never," she answered. "This is my third spread like this one. I have one more to go. It gives me something to do while I wait for my husband's meetings to end." At 3:30 when our meeting was over, she was still quietly stitching away.

Intuitives could embroider a bedspread if they had some way to engage their minds at the same time—like designing the pattern as they work, listening to tapes, TV, or conversing—but they'd probably tackle only one of a kind.

❏ Do you like to see visible results of your work?

Sensing Direction

People with a well-developed sensing preference rarely get lost—or at least they rarely admit they're lost. "I'm just finding a new way home," Jim will say. Sensing people may choose an alternate route just to get there quicker, whereas intuitives will choose a different way for variety.

When someone gives them directions, sensing people seem to be able to form a mental diagram in their mind—like a map—and they don't even need to write down the directions. Intuitives can hear directions twice, write them down, and still get mixed up. (That's me! I always allow 30 minutes extra to get lost.)

Recently I enjoyed hearing a sensing person give directions. With no hesitation he said, "Go one mile and a quarter. Turn left at the third light. You'll see a service station across the street. Follow the paved road to a stop sign. Take a right, which is Route 14. You'll cross a railroad track, then go down a hill and over a one-lane bridge. Turn left at the big red barn. About three-quarters of a mile you'll find their house. Second on the right. It has a white picket fence." So exact. ". . . You can't miss it"—they always add that.

When people ask directions from an intuitive, the person is apt to reply, "Let's see now, I'm not very good on giving directions. I know how to get there but can't tell you. I'll just lead you there; it will be quicker." Some intuitives even have to think which is their right hand.

❏ Do you possess a good sense of direction?

By now you probably know whether or not sensing fact-gathering is your preference. Of course, everyone has to do physical things to survive, but liking them and tolerating them are quite different.

Sensing people operate with common sense to keep the rest of the world's feet planted securely on the ground. Often sensing people and their contributions are taken for granted—as though anyone could do what they do. Others can produce and serve, organize, build, maintain, and beautify, but not with the expertise and ease of a person who prefers the sensing process by God's design. For this reason, learning to understand and appreciate sensing people is important.

Appreciating Sensing People

Since the majority of the world prefers the sensing process, understanding and appreciating their particular contributions and problems will ease tensions in every home, church, business, and school.

"Understanding is a fountain of life to those who have it," says Proverbs 16:22. Understanding and appreciating how God designed minds and hands to work is part of the background of this declaration, since we are social beings whose biggest assignment is to adjust to one another. "I'd rather marry someone with common sense than someone with a million dollars," a veteran wife of 20 years declared.

I hope the following X-ray of the sensing preference will encourage many to square their shoulders and say, "What a feather in my cap! I have much to offer. Not everyone can do what I do easily." I trust that those who live and work with people who prefer the sensing process will conclude, "How remarkable are God's gifts to this type!"

Observation Specialists

You can count on what sensing people say they have seen, heard, smelled, tasted, or touched because they actually embrace the physical world. Recalling minute details is their inborn talent. Therefore, they are reliable witnesses.

Several years ago our city experienced a rash of fraudulent magazine salespersons. Upon our return home one evening, Julia Beth, our high-school-age daughter, reported such an encounter. A very aggressive female barged into our home, urging Julia Beth to find money somewhere, even if it were only a few dollars, to order a magazine. When Julia Beth insisted there was no cash in the house, the intruder suggested she forge one of our checks. "Your folks won't care," she promised. Quite apprehensive by this time, Julia Beth finally edged the woman out the door. When we heard the story, we called the police immediately.

"Can you describe the woman?" the officer questioned. Julia Beth spieled off such a complete description of the suspect's physical appearance, actions, and intricate details of her attire—down to "the middle button was missing from her tan corduroy jacket, the left strap on her brown shoe was frayed, her red nail polish was chipped"—that we were amazed as well as amused. The policeman scratched his head in unbelief as he recorded more than a dozen such details. "We need to put you on the force," he mused. Sensing persons observe and can recall facts like these with little effort.

It is wise to ask sensing persons their opinions about color coordination, materials, and such, because generally they are gifted with decorating expertise. Knowing that they enjoy observing the physical world, indulge their descriptive conversation about what they've seen or heard. Be patient with sensing travelers, especially during season changes. They slowly drink in scenic drives, carefully scanning the fields left and right. I've seem them stop in the middle of a country road to get a closer look at or to listen to a bunch of piglets.

Sensing is essential to enjoying the glories of sunrise, crashing of surf on the beach, aromas of fresh-baked bread, the feel of velour, the flavors of ice cream, and the movements of an athlete. Sensing people enjoy life, savoring it moment by moment.

Master Computer for Facts

The sensing types have a fascination for solid facts and insistence on accurate figures. Because sensing people would rather have all the facts before they act, they are strong in common sense—or "horse sense," as some call it. However, they may lack foresight if their past experience fails to supply case-in-point references. Also, sensing persons can carry doom and gloom into the present if their past experiences have dealt them heavy, negative blows.

Their aptness for accuracy especially qualifies them for detailed work—clerical responsibilities, money handling, measuring, distribution. They are patient checkers and examiners. You can expect sensing people to be reluctant to admit that their facts are incorrect or insufficient. They really think their eyes and ears have caught it all unless one can supply adequate, credible proof to the contrary. Their total trust in their preferred way of gathering data causes them to appear to be quite stubborn and closed-minded at times.

Sometimes fact-loving people believe that they have collected all possible data, not realizing that some very important facts are not set out in black and white but come from possibilities. When arguing with a sensing person, especially if you're an intuitive, determine from the beginning that your sketchy facts and possibility-thinking will be no match for the recall of the actual facts. An intuitive's ideas and reasons may make marvelous sense to some, but will rarely convince a sensing person.

Mix Fact-Gathering

At the parsonage for our church the availability of an open telephone line is often restricted. So several years ago, perturbed at having to wait, Jim threatened to get a second line installed. I immediately reacted adversely, based on the hassle of even one phone.

He meant business, however, and the next thing I knew the deacons had approved moving an extension of the church line into our residence. Jim discounted all my possibility arguments about the inconvenience and confusion of two phones ringing at the same time, violation of what little privacy we have, and on and on. But he wouldn't be persuaded.

Finally, in desperation, I neatly typed and numbered the few benefits of having a second line, and beside them I listed all the drawbacks, and then presented the complete list to Jim without comment. The result? I never heard another word about a second line. I discovered that sensing people will indeed consider emotional reasons when they are listed alongside common-sense facts.

I smugly assumed I had changed his mind until a few months later when again he was tapping his foot impatiently for the phone. "I'm going to put a second line in this house," he muttered. "Want me to pull out my list?" I threatened. I learned a second lesson, that Jim hadn't changed his mind after all; he had merely tabled his idea until the time that I would wise up to his way of thinking.

When dealing with sensing people, endeavor to give accurate data about how much you spent, who you saw, what time it happened, the name of the place, and so on. Also, remember that they prefer to receive facts in chronological order. Intuitives prefer to ask the questions for which they want answers. Give intuitives facts before they want them, and they'll reject them or not hear them.

Avoid rushing sensing people to make decisions before they have all the fixed facts or before they have had time to mull them over. Those who prefer to make sensing, warmhearted decisions will vacillate into guilt or confusion, and those who rely on sensing, cold-logic decisions will react under pressure with a "no." Sensing people, whether using heart or head, like to think things over thoroughly.

Money Matters

Intuitives can handle money and keep financial records when they have to. However, the process drains them more than it does sensing folk. Intuitives might be attracted to finance, accounting, and bookkeeping, but they may become bored by the whole process once they have learned it. Sensing people, on the other hand, enjoy the repetition and dealing with figures. When a sensing person and an intuitive are mates, allowing the sensing person to keep the books balanced is a wise decision. When both are sensing, the one who enjoys it the most or who has the most time may be the best choice.

I have much confidence in Jim's math calculations. I can do that kind of work, but not as accurately or quickly as he. Nor do I enjoy it as much. He takes care of our bookwork and oversees my financial recordkeeping. I resented his condescending attitude toward my figuring ability, but once we understood that our abilities lie in opposite areas, his attitude changed to benevolence and mine to appreciation. While I have access to his expertise, I'll gladly allow him to advise and teach me. I'll willingly handle one of his counseling sessions in exchange for his figuring out my income tax. He would welcome the swap, too.

Past Experience

"I make it a practice never to lend money to my relatives," Pete declared. "I've been burnt a couple of times."

"I'll lend you money for a car," Angy's mother promised, "but on the condition that you keep this one for at least three years. That means you'll have to take very good care of it," she lectured.

Intuitives are more likely to forget past bad debtors and to look at each situation as brand new with no strings attached. Naturally, neither attitude —closed or open-minded—is always right or best. Sensing people consider all the past financial facts before launching into new ones, which is not a bad thing for intuitives to consider.

"Money is something I save," Dwight declared. "But money is something my wife, Alice, uses. She never knows exactly how much she has, but always manages somehow to scrape up enough to do or buy what she thinks she needs."

"I never cash one check until I have another in hand," Rena said quietly. "You never know what's going to happen. I like to save for a rainy day. I have to hide it from Dick, though, because he says money is to use, not to hoard." These snatches of conversation illustrate the difference between the intuitive's and the sensing's regard for money.

Sensing persons make excellent organizational treasurers, clerks, and salespersons. They are usually on top of ordering needed supplies. However, many of these inconspicuous services are rarely praised or acknowledged. Perhaps we can all be more aware of the stabilizing contributions of sensing people.

Rule-Keepers

Sensing people are very observant of rules. If the hospital visiting hours end at 8:30 and they arrive at 8:40, they will usually consider it too late to visit. If the sign reads "No Parking" or "No Smoking," they will generally obey. Others, in contrast, bend rules when needed, assuming the rules apply to others. Sensing people not only follow directions and obey signs, but they also expect others to do likewise. Often intuitives don't even see the signs or the clock.

One time there were ten of us who stopped for ice cream where there was no room for all to sit together. However, I spotted adequate seating in a "Closed Area" and turned around the sign, which read "Birthday Party" on the other side. Our group followed me in. As we chatted around the tables, one of the ladies said, "I wonder why we're the only ones back here?" I disclosed that the area was reserved for birthday parties. "Did you get permission?" she asked. "No, I didn't need to," I said. She was appalled to think we were violating rules. "We're having a party, aren't we? And it's busy, isn't it?" I reasoned. "Well, I guess so," she stammered, still uncomfortable with rule-bending.

Sensing Children

Much of school is geared primarily for sensing children. Little daydreaming is permitted; rather, rote memory and passing facts back and forth abound. Intuitive students catch a fact, and their minds swirl into the wild blue yonder as they envision ways they can put the fact into meaningful operation.

Sensing children usually prefer factual math, history, and general science over theoretical subjects. Filling in the blanks, doing true and false or multiple-choice questions would appeal to the sensing more than the writing of a paragraph. Intuitives are likely to read more into objective questions and consequently invite mental confusion.

By the time children reach 7th grade, their types can be identified with a useful degree of accuracy by employing the Myers-Briggs Type Indicator. Elementary children are still primarily sensing, and fortunately for them, mostly sensing teachers are attracted to elementary teaching. This is good since repetition and routine—and patience on the teacher's part—are so great a part of basic learning.

Sensing parents are less likely to release their children to go to yonder parts of the world because they don't want distance to interrupt traditional family holiday celebrations. When grown children realize their parents are sensing, they can ease the separation with pictures, detailed letters, and regular phone calls that include descriptions of the weather, physical circumstances, new foods, and such. Generally, sensing people are not avid letter writers unless a lot of interesting and different things have happened on which they can report. Sensing people enjoy any method of picking up news—telephone, visits, letters.

Intuitives need notes and letters because they are so apt to forget facts they hear. Keeping a pencil and pad by the phone or in one's purse or pocket is not a bad idea for those unexpected phone calls that substitute for letters.

Maintaining the World

Everyone uses the sensing process to some degree, but trusting and enjoying it is reserved for those who prefer it by God's choice. Our world would be very inconvenient and uncomfortable without sensing people who keep hospitals staffed, machines running, food and supplies prepared and distributed, grounds and buildings maintained, businesses and institutions administrated, finances checked, and life on a common-sense track. These people are very loyal to institutions, clubs, and teams.

"A slack hand causes poverty, but the hand of the diligent makes rich," says Proverbs 10:4. Because sensing people are so comfortable and satisfied with their ability to do things with their hands, where they are in complete control, they are often naïve about dealing with the complex abstract part of life that involves relationship problems, research, and what might be. Avoid dumping relationship problems on sensing minds because producing solutions to emotional problems requires abstract, otherworld thinking, which they do not prefer.

Since they are product-physical-world-oriented, sensing people have an easier time being happy because they are not easily bored. Intuitives are ever needing to be challenged and fulfilled in an abstract way, so therefore they wrestle with restlessness.

Retrospection Authority

Sensing parents are likely to consult the past for pointers and use "when I was your age . . ." reasons for rules and discipline. True, experience is the best teacher, but it is not the sole instructor. Intuitives are equipped to see outcomes without using past experience, so their abstract possibility-thinking is crucial in discipline. But when sharing the discipline of children with a sensing mate, an intuitive should not discount the value of drawing wisdom from past experiences, but instead resist being limited to what happened last time, which prevents growth and improvement. Sensing parents will go with things that have worked in the past, whereas intuitive parents generally go for ideas they feel will work.

Sensing types tend to look at past sorrow and see no hope for the future. Much doom and gloom come from projecting the future on the basis of past experiences. If the past has been disappointing, the prospects for the future will be grim.

Sensing persons, especially introverts who have a pessimistic outlook, will avoid a confrontation, remembering that a heated argument occurred the last time a particular subject was brought up. Sensing types tend to close doors when relationships fail. "It's hard to believe that someone who has hurt me and even asked forgiveness will not hurt me gain," Ellen said. Sensing people just want more guarantees.

For instance, sensing persons who have failed once at cooking rice are inclined to conclude they cannot make rice. Intuitives may forget what food was ruined, only to remember after another failure. Sensing types gather from their reservoir of experiences and may come to seem intuitive, especially if they live many years.

Factual Communicators

"I don't understand men," a young wife confessed recently. "Will I ever? At home, Gus is glum. But let someone drop in, and he's full of humor, charm, and information."

Why is Gus glum at home? He needs facts in common to encourage conversation. He and his wife haven't worked together, so going over the day's experiences isn't easy, although it's possible. His buddy says, "I see you bought a new van. What kind of mileage does it get?" This automatically spawns conversation.

"If I don't say anything in the car, no one talks," Martha complained. "Mark is mute unless he's talking about football."

"I learn more about my husband by listening to him talk on the phone than by what he says directly to me," Thelma pouted. "I feel so shut out."

Sensing mates need facts to discuss, questions to answer, and topics to be introduced. Boredom or competition needlessly affects thousands of marriages because it goes unidentified. Because sensing people rely heavily on experiences and known facts for conversation, unless exciting things happen —such as births, promotions, moves, operations, or travel—they become bored. However, they can learn to create projects and to draw people into their lives to keep conversation rolling.

Since the majority of the world prefers sense fact-finding, most marriages are between sensing people. When mates share this process, they have an easier time getting along. But conversation usually wears thin in about seven to ten years. Since they are short on intuition, they will lack new ideas about where to go and what to do. Solutions to the relationship problems that increase as children grow older are likely to be difficult to find. This explains why many parents encourage their children to live close to home, so that they can provide friendship and variety and subjects to discuss. However, this close association with parents can keep children from discovering their own special design and gifts from God.

To stimulate communication, a sensing mate could learn to ask questions such as: "With whom did you eat lunch?" "What did you discuss?" "Did anyone get hurt today?" "Was the boss in a good mood?" "Who is about to retire?" "Have you seen John Green lately? How's his leg?" This is consulting the intuitive process. Intuitive people can think of a million questions to ask. This doesn't happen to be the gift of sensing people. Consequently, intuitives can draw people out, even when their experiences have little in common.

This is how John Miller described a typical Friday night conversation between him and his wife, both sensing people who have been married eight years.

"What do you want to do tonight, Janeen?"

"I don't know. What do you want to do, John?"

"I have no preference. Want to go out to eat?"

"Yeah, that's okay. Whatever you want."

"Where would you like to go?"

"It doesn't matter to me, any place."

"Let's go to Wendy's."

"Okay."

This couple's resources are limited unless they develop their possibility-thinking. To avoid boredom or deadlock on where to go or what to do, two sensing people might do the following:

•Purposefully bring people into their lives and home—guaranteed conversation.

•Get involved in church and community affairs—guaranteed maintaining, conserving, and building projects.

•Remodel a home together, work a garden, or restore a car.

•Write out different suggestions of places to go, people to visit, things to do, and on an agreed day each week draw out one suggestion and act on it.

This last idea has been especially successful. "Sounds like fun," said Jack, a bored 45-year-old husband. "I'd like to draw the slip on Thursday, though," his wife, Ramona, suggested, "So I could do a little planning and look forward to it."

Sensing people prefer one fact at a time. "Don't confuse me with so many ideas at once," Fred resisted. "But I've got to empty out my mind," Janet pleaded. "My mental computer has a one-item-at-a-time capacity, so write your ideas out for consideration."

Fred's solution was wise. It is easy to clog a sensing person's mind, which likes to examine every aspect. Listing myriad, and often fuzzy, abstract facts on paper helps to clarify as well as modify mental entanglements and reduce disagreements. When sensing persons read an intuitive's list, they may accept several possibilities that will influence the final decision. Dealing with people according to their individual perception not only surmounts great barriers in a relationship, but also is a high compliment to them.

Jim, for instance, likes to tell about a conference he has attended from start to finish, describing the speakers in the order that he heard them. If I interrupt his chronological account with questions, he'll say, "Just let me finish, then ask questions." That means I have to make mental notes of my questions. Since I forget quickly, often I jot down a note or two while Jim recounts so we can back up for my particular people-details.

Sensing people respond to factual conversation, so if you're trying to keep them awake or interested while driving, read or talk about something that appeals to this type of mind. Short stories or factual articles are a good source. Sensing people respect a fact more if it has been written in a book than if you have thought it up. Abstractions must have plenty of support before they are taken seriously.

Production

Sensing people appreciate knowing that their product—a homemade bookshelf, a meal, whatever—meets a need more than they appreciate hearing, "You're so wonderful to do that for me." They love for their work to be admired. Appreciate and use what a senser does for you and gives you, and you have appreciated the person. Their desire to produce pushes them to work long, tedious hours in the kitchen, at the sewing machine, or in the operating room, factory, garden, gym, or practice room.

Sometimes in an unhappy marriage sensing mates can increase the amount of handwork to ensure a reliable source of accomplishment, happiness, and self-esteem, rather than having to draw it from their spouse. Because much of their self-esteem is connected to their products and services, filling needs and meeting standards are their goals.

Lovers of Repetition

Because sensing people like repetition, they particularly enjoy routine, especially if they are structured. They are likely to clean house on the same day and in the same manner—starting in the kitchen, for instance. They sing a traditional song:

> Today is Monday,
> Monday washday,
> Everybody happy?
> Well, I must say.
>
> Today is Tuesday.
> Tuesday ironing day,
> Everybody happy?
> Well, I must say, . . .

Intuitives have a strategy, but will begin scrubbing the kitchen floor in a different spot each time just to change the routine. Intuitives prefer variable routine, but sensing persons develop a system they like and repeat it. Intuitives don't really enjoy housework the way sensing people do. They prefer problem-solving, which sensing people dislike.

"I'd much rather clean someone else's house than listen to all her personal problems," Ellen said. "At least when you're finished with the house you can see some accomplishment." Sensing people prefer to render physical care, and thus admire the intuitives who are willing to listen and talk to needy persons about personal and family problems.

Traditionally, women have been relegated to sensing occupations. Now we understand why some women wanted release so badly. But sensing people should not be criticized for enjoying a mundane or repetitive job, as though it requires no mind whatever.

Since Jim and I are now more conscious of each other's innate preferences, my guilt has subsided when I'm not as competent as he in hands-on projects.

Recently Jim laid a slate entrance to our living room. With great patience he cemented each piece to the floor, then began to fill the grooves with grout. What tedious work! He even admitted it was a drag. I felt sorry for him and wondered how he could bear to stoop for such long periods.

Knowing he felt pressure from his schedule because the project was requiring more time than he had allowed, I said, "I have an hour free right now, could I help do that?" "No thanks," he said quickly. "I have time to do it, but not time to re-do it." That statement might have hurt my feelings a couple of years ago, because I believe I can do anything as well as anyone else if I put my mind to it. But Jim knows—and I know—that my patience lies with people—not grout. If he had taken me up on my offer, I don't know what I would have said. I don't really like to get my hands dirty. However, I did help by bringing him rags, screening phone calls, praising his work, and encouraging him.

If possible, sensing people need plenty of warning when a change is coming, because they prefer that the events of the day fall pretty much like the day before.

"Everyday is different at work," Claudia shared. "I never know whether I'll be working upstairs or down, with papers or products. This keeps me on edge all the time because I never feel I accomplish anything. I like to see evidence of my labor. And I like to know exactly what I'm supposed to do." Claudia's boss was glad to grant an adjustment in responsibilities that changed her entire attitude toward her employment and eliminated her chronic headaches.

Be patient with the sensors' toleration as well as enjoyment of repetition. Appreciate their products and services without taking for granted the tedious, backbreaking hours of preparing and repairing.

Direction Conscious

I feel safer when traveling with sensing persons because they seem able to read maps easier and figure out how to return. The mass of highways interchanging with exit and entrance ramps in every direction totally confuses my limited-sensing mind. One time an intuitive friend of mine and I drove 50 miles in the wrong direction, and if we hadn't had car trouble, we would have gone even farther.

Sensing persons usually know more about repairing a car or correcting a wrong turn on the eight-laner. I appreciate Jim's expertise in this area and feel a bit apprehensive when I travel without him, his maps, and trusty toolbox.

When I get behind the wheel, I say to myself: "You are now consulting your sensing process. Notice the traffic lights, watch the street names and numbers, keep your mind on what you are doing. Be aware of the speedometer and the gas gauge, as well as any little red lights that may come on."

Conclusion

The entire book of Proverbs is a common-sense book offering encouragement to work with the hands, be observant of the world around, learn from past experiences, develop good habits, and accept counsel from those who are wise. Sensing people have little difficulty with these things; but solving relationship problems, looking ahead, avoiding possible difficulties, and dealing with abstract ideas are the areas in which sensing people need to consult their intuition, as well as their intuitive friends and acquaintances.

People who are good with their hands may regard those who are all thumbs as untalented, inept, or lazy, but those who are gifted in the sensing process preference are not superior to those who prefer the intuitive process. They are just different.

Respecting the two ways of gathering facts and information requires humility and patience, but it produces creative compromise that guarantees smooth-running relationships—the basic desire of everyone, especially God. Without physical work to do, crafts to finish, golf to play, books to read, budgets to balance, TV to watch, projects to work on, or grandchildren to entertain, sensing people will be unfilled.

In our bicycle hike, sensing people are easy to spot because their conservatively painted 10-speeds are equipped with all the gadgets—generator lights, horns, comfortable seats, sturdy handle grips, toe-fitting pedals, reflectors, speedometers, passenger carriers, and large baskets loaded with lunch boxes, rain gear, repair kits, and first-aid supplies. The riders have cameras slung over their shoulders and transistor radios to keep up with the weather and news. Their jackets often bear the name of an organization, business, or group.

Lord, give me courage to move out of my comfort zone sometimes and attempt something new. Enable me to catch a vision of possibilities for my life.

Notes

[1]Isabel Briggs Myers and Peter B. Myers, *Gifts Differing* (Palo Alto CA: Consulting Psychologists Press, 1980) 201.

[2]Keirsey and Marilyn Bates, *Please Understand Me* (Del Mar CA: Prometheus Nemesis Books, 1978) 17.

Chapter 6

Idea and Possibility People

To get wisdom is to love oneself; to keep understanding is to prosper.
—Proverbs 19:8

How much better to get wisdom than gold! To get understanding is to be chosen rather than silver.
—Proverbs 16:16

The second way of gathering information is through intuition, which is the faculty for knowing without the use of rational processes—or immediate cognition. It is the capacity for guessing accurately or for having sharp insight.

"I had always felt rather weird, and now I know why," Pat shared. "Inside I knew how difficult it was to try to be like everyone else, but I kept apologizing for how differently my mind worked. How relieved I am to find out that a few others think just like I do and have experienced the same wonderings. Why, I feel like a brand new person with a new lease on life!" Pat prefers intuition by God's design. Approximately 25 percent of the population can identify with her preference for gathering facts and information through perception of possibilities.

Because intuition is abstract, a preference for it is often difficult to identify until later in life. In the words of Myers: "The intuitive child born into a very matter-of-fact family, who has no time for books and no talk about anything except obvious realities, will go half-fed.[1]

The love for books and learning ideas automatically drives people toward higher education. There, in the college scene, intuitives are likely to meet a concentration of people like themselves. Unfortunately, some intuitives never have positive exposure to another intuitive and thus believe they are inferior and even lacking in intelligence.

Profile of an Intuitive

While sensing people rely on their senses for gathering facts, intuitives gather information from the unknown world or the imagination—things that haven't happened yet. They have the distinct ability to project what might happen without having experienced a sample situation. If they are introverted, they are likely to project pessimistic outcomes, and if extroverted, expect optimistic possibilities.

Intuitives use actual sensing facts primarily to back up their hunches and to have more trust in their vibes than in what they see, hear, smell, touch, or taste. Facts merely become steppingstones toward solutions.

Many intuitive people lack self-esteem because making or doing things with their hands does not bring the satisfaction that it does to sensing people. Unless their intangible offerings of ideas, solutions, and designs are recorded on paper, displayed on canvas, acted out, or presented in lectures or music, their lives have limited meaning. Until someone appreciates their mental contributions, intuitives feel inadequate and lack a sense of purpose. As one intuitive quipped, "My self-esteem is so low that I have to reach up to hit bottom. Instead of coping, I've been groping."

"I've lived my whole life on the service road," April analyzed. "Now that I know the idea world is normal, I've been released to enjoy the freeway of God's design for me. Intuition is part of my new song to Jesus that he gave me and that I will, by his grace, sing to him in all its variations as he makes it more melodious and harmonious in the coming years," she continued.

Because children are first taught physical survival, our primary beginnings are more sensing than intuitive. Then, because parents attempt to mold their children after themselves, people often do not discover until they reach midlife that doing things with their hands is an option rather than an absolute. So, distinguishing children's—or one's own—intuitive preference is not easy if our ideas and creativity have been squelched. But, if undisturbed, intuitives will naturally migrate toward innate preferences.

Since females seem able to consult their intuitive process with more ease than men, woman's intuition is a recognized power (or plague), especially in marriage relationships. Because women tend to have many insightful hunches, some have difficulty ascertaining which fact-gathering process is really their favorite. For instance, one of my close female friends dislikes reading maps, has a poor sense of direction, and is impatient with repairing mechanical things. Yet she says she fits snugly into all the other sensing preferences. She is a product, routine, repetition, fact, and detail person—and she loves it. Her close identification with the intuitive preference stems from God's special dose to women. Keep this in mind as you evaluate yourself.

Ideas, Ideas

Intuitives gather abstract possibilities as easily as sensing people collect facts. In fact, intuitives are likely to accept their thoughts as bonafide actuality. Contrary to what some people suppose, intuitives have not just become lazy about facts and drifted to intuition. God just gave them a healthier respect for concepts than for physical facts and figures. Believe me, their minds are stuffed full of ideas—with several stampeding to be expressed by hand or mouth at the same time.

Most intuitives are really surprised to learn that not everyone possesses scads of ideas. "For years I never gave anyone my ideas," Lillian said, "because I thought everyone already had them. 'Why am I suggesting to people obvious solutions?' I would reason. But now I know my ideas are not common, although they seem very ordinary to me."

Some intuitives become very defensive regarding their casual treatment of facts. "I respect collecting all the facts," a male intuitive defended. "You just think you have all the data," I chided. "If you get to the point where you don't have some needed fact, you'll make up one right on the spot, won't you?" He smiled and admitted that was true. "But my made-up one usually turns out to be quite accurate," he added. "I see no reason for having extra facts that you're not going to use. What a waste! I'd rather dig up some than have a few too many."

Intuitives figure that it is better not to clutter the mind by memorizing facts when they can consult a file with all that information (they just have to know where the file is). "I just want to keep my brain available for important stuff rather than a lot of trivial facts that I call 'superfluous trash,'" Ralph exclaimed.

For intuitives, every new fact opens the door for a possibility—and they love possibilities. Because intuitives are teeming with ideas, they have to jot them down so not to lose them. Writing intuitives may keep pencil and pad on their nightstands for midnight inspirations.

❏ Do you prefer gathering ideas and reasons over collecting facts?

Analyzers

Intuitives prefer to skim physical facts so that they can get on with people-and-systems analysis. They are constantly asking or finding reasons for everything they or anyone else says or does. They cannot rest until they have full explanations. They may ask: "Why are you doing it that way?" "How come you . . .?" "What would happen if . . .?" "Have you ever thought of . . .?"

Young intuitives take watches and clocks apart, like sensing children, but for different reasons. Sensing children want to see how timepieces work and then fix them; intuitive children want to see why they work and then perhaps improve the workings.

"Why do you always question me about what I decided to do?" Jim used to ask me. "I feel like you are giving me the third degree and trying to poke holes in my judgment." Many years elapsed before Jim even verbalized this complaint and several more before he was convinced that my intentions were not meant to be critical or to question his judgment, but to analyze all the possibilities. Had I known I was an intuitive, many misunderstandings and hurt feelings would have been avoided. I condemned myself unmercilessly for being a super judgmental person, though what I saw in my mind was as plain as day to me. Fortunately, we both learned to understand and appreciate my inner vision and see what a great asset it was, especially in dealing with people and their relationships and emotional adjustments and for finding alternatives in other situations.

Since intuitives have a gift for putting two and two together, they are often drawn to sharing ideas through counseling, writing, speaking, and teaching. Introverted thinking intuitives, who are less people-oriented, may be more comfortable with one-on-one or analysis and design of systems. Relying on cold logic, they can usually handle complex mathematical calculations, philosophical ideas, and theories.

❏ Are you drawn to people or systems problem-solving?

Alive to the Abstract World

Observable facts do not attract intuitives as they do sensing people, but intuitives can turn their minds to physical observations and processes when necessary—for example, when operating a vehicle. But a physical exercise drains them pretty quickly. Intuitives miss a lot with the eye and ear because their minds are preoccupied with abstract ideas. Therefore, at times intuitives are likely to be labeled by family and acquaintances as air-headed, addled, flaky, out of their tree, hazy-headed, spacey, scatterbrained, and off the wall. The proverbial absent-minded professor certainly falls into this category.

Once, as I waited my turn at the hair salon, I relaxed on the circular lounge totally engrossed in examining my personal calendar, I became conscious of glances my way. "Am I dressed appropriately?" I wondered. I was astonished to follow the animated smiles and pointing to a life-sized rag doll on which I was actually half leaning. Not only had I not noticed it, but I had not felt it, either. Intuitives see only what they look for, as some people who listen for a certain answer or hear only what they expect to hear.

My family teases me about being a "Mars" mother, so involved in writing early one morning that I was unaware our tiny kitten had crawled up on my head. Intuitives can become so absorbed in mental gymnastics that they do not smell food burning, hear alarms, or realize they are hungry, cold, or hot. Many miss road signs and signal lights—even red ones.

"I'm so glad to find out that I'm normal," Ginny sighed. "My husband has been accusing me of having a screw loose. I try to see and hear everything, but no matter how hard I try, I still miss a lot. Don't ask me to describe how someone was dressed or the décor of a home. I could do it if I purposely said to myself, 'Now notice what you see,' but it is not natural for me. I don't miss what people say, though." Intuitives may see around corners, but miss considerations right under their noses.

❑ Are you keenly aware of the abstract world?

Resistant to Fixed Physical Routine

Because intuitives are full of ideas and planning tomorrow, bored with facts and what's happening today, an open schedule attracts them more than a fixed routine. For example, a sensing person may find security in punching a time clock every day for years, while an intuitive would feel quite uncomfortable with this schedule. Intuitives may prefer to fit in their eight hours when it is convenient for them or makes better mental sense.

Intuitives work just as hard as sensing people, but their delights and achievements are not always visible. The intuitive mind doesn't grind like a machine, nor can ideas be stacked in boxes. Most intuitives would rather spend three hours analyzing a situation or discussing a person's problem than one hour painting a fence, operating a machine, or sewing quilt squares.

Sometimes sensing people regard intuitives as a lazy bunch because they always seem to be trying to get out of physical labor. They don't enjoy making things or rendering physical service as much as they enjoy designing products or solving problems.

Intuitive homemakers agree that cleaning house, washing, and ironing do not merit top priority on their list of things to do. However, they perform these duties out of obligation, mixed with delight in wanting improvement, along with a desire to maintain their reputation. Sensing people generally clean one room at a time—from the top down—whereas intuitives clean the whole house at the same time. "I spend lots of time hunting for where I left the furniture cream," Ellen admitted.

Even spontaneous intuitive persons who prefer the outdoors dislike physical routine. "My wife hates to see me cut the grass," Wilbur grinned. "She cuts it straight up and down—back and forth—I like to make circles, squares, triangles, and fill them in. If I can't do it differently each time and make a game of it, I can't stand to do it at all."

❏ Does fixed physical routine bore you?

Repelled by Repetition

Intuitives love variety. In fact, repetition will drive most intuitives crazy, and once they've learned a job, they'll look for a new one to conquer. Many intuitives have shared that once they learned how to add, subtract, multiply, and divide, doing an entire page of the same type of problem was frustrating. In an effort to get through that kind of tedium, they often hurried their work and made dumb mistakes.

Excitedly, I opened the package with the photograph album, already anticipating placing the pile of snapshots in plastic windows. However, when I discovered that the pages would need the holes punched out before fitting them on the notebook rings, I thought, "Yuk," and stuffed the photos back into the envelope. Later when Jim inspected the contents, without a word he got the ice pick and punched out all those little holes. He enjoyed the repetitious project that would have bored me silly.

"Although Harry is an expert mechanic, I was hurt when he instructed me to get the garage man to change my spark plugs and oil if I wanted it done," Grace said. "I thought he was neglecting me and wasting money, too. But now I understand that for him to do tune-up jobs would be like his expecting me to find solutions to someone's marriage problems. Harry said because there was no way to improve on changing oil and since we could afford the service, he couldn't be bothered anymore."

Intuitives do not particularly enjoy handwork unless it involves learning all the various types, mastering each, and then designing new ones. When intuitives do crafts, they will probably mix in other mental involvements—listening to tapes, watching TV, or conversing. After I learned how to knit I couldn't stand just to quietly knit, so I usually read a book or listened to the radio at the same time. Intuitives love to "kill two birds with one stone."

One of my friends says the thing she likes best about remote control on TV is that it allows her to watch two or three shows at one time. She detests reruns and commercials.

❏ Are you easily bored with repetition and need variety?

Goal Setting

When intuitives head for a goal, they'll stumble over facts and even people to get there, assuming everyone is the same. They require a challenge, or else their reason for doing or being is null and void. When intuitives reach a goal, however, they may lose all incentive to continue. Amassing wealth does not usually serve as sufficient challenge for intuitives. They want to succeed, not for the money, but for recognition.

"Ed has climbed the economic ladder twice now, only to fall into restlessness and alcoholism," Denise said hopelessly. "It makes no difference how much money he makes, he can't seem to handle reaching his financial goals. Unless he's continually challenged mentally, he's bored to death and feels worthless."

Since intuitives have a tendency to gravitate toward higher learning, many find at midlife that they have degrees in contrasting fields. For this reason they are often thought of as professional students. So many subjects fascinate them that they may not know what they want to spend most of their time doing. They even have difficulty deciding what hobby, sport, or pastime is their favorite.

❏ Are you dissatisfied without a challenging goal?

Challenged by Recognition

"David has been in hog heaven since he was promoted to manager," Carol shared. "There is no increase in pay, but he has a nameplate and a desk. He really doesn't care that his paycheck doesn't reflect his new position yet. The boss likes his ideas; that's all that matters to him. He projects that he will be in charge of the place in a few years."

Intuitives would rather be someone than have something. They represent primarily themselves rather than a company or group. Educational degrees are important to them, yet they are not particularly impressed by another's position or title as much as by how much that person knows. Making a name is more of a challenge for intuitives than financial success. A good reputation is very important to them.

❏ Are you more concerned with gaining reputation and recognition than physical and financial accomplishments?

Money Matters

Intuitives rarely know exactly how much money they have. Money matters little; they just want enough to buy the things they need. "Money is something I use," an intuitive executive explained. "And math is something I can do, but I'm glad when I don't have to," he continued.

The job of balancing books seldom attracts intuitives; they would rather be involved in things that can be improved, not just recorded. Following bookkeeping and accounting rules would not interest most intuitives after they learned the ropes. Occasionally they may have grandiose plans for getting rich quick, while sensing persons would prefer to plod along doing something lower paying but dependable.

Acquiring possessions may not be as important to intuitives because they are "tomorrow persons" rather than "today persons." Certainly they appreciate comfort, nice clothes, and pleasant surroundings, but since the majority of their satisfaction does not come through their eyes and ears, they can take or leave these things.

❏ Are you casual about gathering wealth and possessions and keeping track of money?

Vision Decisions

Whereas sensing people rely heavily on past experiences and objective facts for their decision making, intuitives lean on hunches, analysis, and possibility-thinking. Since they are tomorrow-people, intuitives don't rely on past experiences because they tend to forget what happened. Their thoughts and ideas pole-vault current physical facts and barriers and project way into the future. If known facts seem to get in the way of something intuitives want to do, they will ignore the obstacles and somehow find a way. "Never say it can't be done to Karen," Hank said. "That's like saying 'siccum' to a dog. If she needs money for something, she'll rake it up somehow."

Because intuitives jump from one idea to another, they may not realize how far out in left field they've wandered when they finally come to a conclusion. Some people refer to intuitives as dreamers. Sensing facts are critical for wise decisions, but among the intuitives' dozens of alternatives and possibilities often lie the most economical and efficient, practical and brilliant suggestions.

❏ Do you trust possibility-thinking when making decisions?

Idea Conversation

Because intuitives are so interested in ideas, they make good conversationalists. Because of their complex minds and possibility thinking, they can dream up 20 questions in 20 seconds. Extroverted, feeling intuitives are especially good at drawing people out—even the very private ones. They are also skilled in expressing themselves.

Because intuitives think of several answers to one question, they may offer fragmented answers. They may not complete sentences because another thought is straining for expression. Intuitives may even forget their last comment.

For example, if I ask Jim a question that requires some thought on his part, often by the time he answers it my mind has flitted on to another area, and I have to ask him what the question was. Sometimes I will make a statement that draws only a strange, inquisitive look from him. "What are you talking about?" he'll ask disgustedly. "Without realizing it, I will have completed some thought in my head and changed subject matter without informing him.

Intuitives enjoy subtle conversation, plays on words, puns, and open-ended tales that require time to guess the outcome.

❏ Are your conversations based on ideas?

Reading

Intuitives love to read, especially in theoretical, philosophical, analytical, and scientific areas. Sometimes this insatiable love for learning intimidates others. Bruce's family, for instance, accused him of being arrogant and feigning intellectualism when he rejected their reading suggestions. He preferred books they couldn't and didn't care to understand. They dubbed him a snob, but Bruce was anything but a snob. He was merely a private person and a serious student. Intuitives alienate others without realizing it or intending to, coming across as know-it-alls.

❏ Do you enjoy reading about human behavior and how the universe functions?

Writing

Intuitives enjoy putting their thoughts and ideas on paper. They like to keep journals and diaries. Introverted intuitives enjoy writing more than speaking, whereas extroverted intuitives are comfortable lecturing, leading groups, and expressing ideas vocally. I taught school for twelve years and was happy, but I have never been happier than in counseling and writing.

❏ Do you enjoy writing and/or counseling?

If you checked most of the preceding boxes, you may conclude that God gifted you with the intuitive preference. Now the world needs to learn how to understand and appreciate you.

Appreciating Intuitives

Keep in mind that everyone is a blend of both sensing and intuition, so there are no pure intuitives—nor would that be feasible. Without a balance of the sensing process, intuitives would lose touch with reality.

Only extreme intuitives can be spotted in their early years. Moderate intuitives tend to be concrete in their behavior and outlook and appear very similar to moderately sensory children. The slow surfacing of the intuitive (N) characteristic in children makes them appear to be few in number, and so extreme intuitives, especially introverted feeling-intuitives, are subject to feeling like "ugly ducklings."[2]

Not only do extremely intuitive children feel like ugly ducklings, but also intuitive adults who have noticed their difference from most of the world have often concluded that they are inferior and inadequate. They have these feelings because they have few physical accomplishments to display, suffer from boredom, appear to be lazy, struggle to find a suitable job, are indecisive, and intimidate others with their natural insight, analysis, and love for learning.

Just as introverts are viewed as bored, unfriendly, sad, or mad, intuitives are often tagged as eggheads, airheads, know-it-alls, scatterbrains, and the like because the complex workings of their minds are shared only by a minority. Intuitives didn't choose their mental makeup any more than sensing people chose theirs, but given a choice, intuitives wouldn't want to trade any more than sensing people would.

I hope these reflections will build self-esteem in intuitives and also engender understanding and appreciation on the part of the common-sense majority segment of society. Discovering each other's gifts certainly can promote peace in all quarters.

Without trying, intuitives are in a constant state of brainstorming. As intriguing facts are presented, their minds go skittering ahead, considering how that knowledge or principle could be put to use. Consequently, they sometimes miss subsequent facts and data, not because they are disinterested, but because they are preoccupied. This insight should help teachers understand those students who often seem to be in another world.

"As I read those stories about the American Indians, I just imagined I was there," Evie reminisced. "I could almost smell the campfires and hear the shrieks of the Indian attackers. I liked to read between the lines as we studied their conquests and defeats. I love the stories of history, but I'm terrible at remembering dates and the names of rivers and explorers. But if you ask me when the War of 1812 was fought, I could tell you right off." Not many intuitives would be able to spiel off their auto license numbers, yet they might be able to quote long passages of prose or poetry.

When handed a sheath of papers or a syllabus, intuitive students will most likely scan, searching out the "chocolate chip" items. Sensing persons, however, will probably start at the beginning and read as the instructor directs. Reading the first page of instructions might be the hardest assignment for intuitives. Give intuitives a technical book and watch them turn to the table of contents first. They like to get an overall view of a subject before they concentrate on individual facts.

Intriguing Possibilities

Like butterflies, intuitives tend to taste every flower, leaving untapped good behind. They are constantly searching out possibilities, and it doesn't take them long to discover whether or not they'll enjoy a certain subject or experience.

Intuitive thinking is helical, or spiral, in form rather than empirical, or moving from observation or experiment, as with sensing thinking. Hence, sensing persons are likely to consider matters quite differently than intuitives. When a sensing person and an intuitive disagree, this presents problems. Because they don't share the same arena, understanding one another's perspective requires creative listening, a facet of humility. Allowing one's spouse or child to have a different viewpoint or opinion paves the way for compromise, a dimension sadly missing in many homes today.

It has been well said that the goal of intuitives is to have a goal or four. "If we don't set goals, we won't know when we get there," an enthusiastic intuitive explained. One extroverted intuitive described his possibility-thinking in this way: "I see a ladder, wide at the bottom, ascending upward. As I near the top, I see another ladder with a wide bottom. My biggest fear is reaching a goal without seeing another ladder."

Extroverted intuitives are likely to see only optimistic possibilities. They pay little attention to past experiences—unless past experiences aid their cause.

Intuitives live primarily in the future. "Your mind is too important to waste it on yesterday," one commented. However, introverted intuitives' ladders are likely to spiral downward toward negative possibilities. Whereas introverted sensing persons might be afraid of physical failure, introverted intuitives fear mental or emotional failure.

Because of their gift for seeing possibilities, intuitives are frequently drawn to counseling careers. Their aptitude for analysis, imagination, and design also draws them to professions such as research, law, writing, ministry, and engineering. Though they have many ideas running through their minds, they may have difficulty deciding what to write about or what particular challenge to meet.

Possibilities intrigue intuitives. They dislike being pinned down to one specific choice because their likes and dislikes change as they try new things and follow challenges.

Intuitives often put themselves down for not being single-minded, but as they discover that their gift is for seeing approaching problems and staying abreast of difficulties, they will learn to appreciate their abstract contributions and thus generate self-esteem.

An individual with the freedom to choose between the sensing or intuitive process in making decisions has to shut down one process to use the other. However, in a marriage between an intuitive and a sensing person, no shutdown is necessary, which allows full benefit from each process. Despite the opposition of intuition and sensing, the two complement each other.

Once on vacation, when I was taking a rare turn at the wheel while the others napped, trouble developed in the rear axle, resulting in a blown tire and a fire in the wheel well. In the few seconds that it took me to manipulate the car and camper to the side of the highway and alert Jim, my mind clicked ahead. "We'll have to ask a motorist to inform our friends in Nashville that we'll be delayed for lunch. Grandma and I can get the lawn chairs from the camper and put them in the shade while Jim and Roger repair the tire. We have plenty to read." Jim was not thinking about possibilities at all. He was thinking about changing that tire—period!

Our predicament was much worse than we imagined, however, because the axle was bent, and replacement would require an overnight delay. While Jim took care of the mechanical problems, I thought ahead to two wedding rehearsals we could never make. After a 24-hour delay, we were on our way. Three hours later a carbon-copy experience occurred with the other axle.

Again, Jim took care of the physical, mechanical end of it with ease while I thought of arrangements we would have to make by phone to find substitutes to perform the weddings and cover for our Sunday school classes and the preaching services on Sunday.

By driving all night, we made it for the second Sunday service, but had we not been opposites, dealing with the emergency situation would have been much more draining for everyone involved. We were both at our best.

Reasons

Intuitives need reasons for doing anything. They question everything. "If someone tells me I'm doing something wrong," Angela exclaimed, "I have to know why."

The "whys" of intuitives drive a sensing mate, parent, or boss up the wall. Sensing people wonder why intuitives want to know why. Sometimes sensing people feel threatened by such questions, which seem to be probing for flaws in their work, judgment, or decisions. This analytical attitude invites contemptuous responses. "Who do they think they are?" "Know-it-alls?" Intuitives just have to learn to live with this.

Intuitives can put sensing friends at ease by assuring them that they are questioning out of interest, not conducting an interrogation. Questions are apt to unnerve those who are not confident about how or why they do things a certain way.

Intuitives play a strategic role in the work world and can threaten experience-trusting, sensing people until this opposite type understands God's design. Reasons make more sense to intuitives than statements of fact. Therefore, sensing people can learn to throw in a few background reasons along with their directions. A convinced intuitive is unstoppable and will produce good quality and quantity when confident things are being done in a reasonable way.

Intuitives can lessen tensions even more by disciplining themselves to ask one question at a time. Jim often asks, "Which question do you want me to answer first?" He understands now that, rather than trying to snow him, I may forget all my questions if I don't verbalize them as they come to mind.

Harnessing the Mind

When intuitives understand how their minds work, they can control their ideas and discipline themselves to concentrate on the subject at hand.

One of my intuitive friends, knowing I am also intuitive, facetiously asked if I ever listened through another's entire verbal prayer. Who likes to admit that even in prayer their mind drifts hither and yon? To harness my mind, my personal praying is most often done with pencil and notebook.

Possibilities never cease for intuitives. Their minds never rest; it's much like mental aerobics going on all the time. Shutting down ideas is easier said than done. Some strong extroverted intuitives report that it's not unusual to have five or six ideas for conversation rushing through their minds at the same time. Some can watch TV, carry on a conversation, plan menus, and have a song running through their head all at the same time. No wonder they don't always make sense, finish sentences, or remember where they are.

When I was substitute teaching, I was appalled more than one time to look up from my writing to face a brand new class. I would have missed the exit of the previous class and the entrance of the new class. My big problem was keeping my surprise a secret.

When sensing persons understand why intuitives tend to be other-worldly, they can assist in organizing their suggestions,. especially in committee meetings. Every committee needs at least one intuitive, but "I think we have enough ideas to go on" is a kind reminder to shut down.

When two intuitives marry, they are likely to be swamped with ideas. "We've instituted an idea time limit," Juanita said. "Otherwise, we're all talk and no action."

Although an intuitive should not endeavor to become a sensing person —one cannot change his or her inborn preferences—the intuitive who completely ignores sensing facts ends up being out of touch with reality. So, learning to respect physical facts will balance an intuitive. On the other hand, an intuitive withers without having fresh thoughts and ideas, just as a plant dies due to lack of sunshine and water. "I get up at 5:30 and do nothing but sit and think for two hours before I go to the truck terminal," Andy confided. "I'd go crazy without that time."

Sleep Patterns

Sensing people have little idea what intuitives, both structured and unstructured, go through to fall off to sleep.

"I have this whirlpool of thoughts that grows into worry competing with sleep," Bruce said. "I try to shut it off, but several more sift immediately on top. The entire time one big thought will loom strongest with many unrelated events or ideas dancing all around. I haven't slept for three nights. I won't until some things are settled at work."

The Martins discovered their mental differences in the wee hours of the morning.

"Can't you please lie still?" Phil griped.

"I just can't go to sleep," Angie apologized.

"What's wrong?"

"Nothing. I just can't turn off my mind."

"Just forget what you're thinking about and go to sleep," Phil counseled.

"Easier said than done," Angie defended. "Tell me what's on *your* mind, Phil."

"Nothing, absolutely nothing except going to sleep."

"I've never had just one thing on my mind—ever," Angie interjected. "Let me tell you all the things that I'm thinking about at the same time."

After Angie rehearsed what was on her mind, Phil gained new appreciation for the difficulty in turning her mind off.

One structured intuitive shared that after she learned the cortex controls the consciousness center, she concentrated on shutting down the cortex. It seemed to help at times. Others say they think of physical relaxation by starting with the toes and working their mental way up the body.

"When I am plagued with so many ideas when I'm trying to sleep," Linda, a structured intuitive executive, said, "I merely turn my light on and write them down. Seems like when I record my ideas, they leave. I imagine the paper is like a safe deposit box."

For many intuitives, drinking warm milk and reading before turning off the light is a necessary ritual.

Mental Mechanics

Intuitives whom I've interviewed agree that they prefer mental over physical mechanics. They regard hands-on jobs as work and mental endeavors as enjoyment or fun. As a rule, intuitives do not relish doing housework, cleaning cars, straightening drawers, painting walls, and the like. Normally they prefer to work toward permanent improvement or change in design, which may explain their switching furniture around quite often. "I enjoy the challenge of setting up office files for someone else to use," Janie said.

Structured intuitives tolerate daily, routine tasks because finishing things gives them at least some measure of satisfaction. I finish physical tasks to earn the right to type a manuscript or write an article, which is more like play to me, but is something in which a sensing person might be tempted to procrastinate.

"I was impressed when Jack enthusiastically tackled our flood-devastated yard, turning it into a beautifully landscaped garden spot," Wilma marveled. "I would have had to study and follow a guide, but he just surveyed the problem visually and did it," she continued. "But at this point it's a bone of contention because he has absolutely no interest in maintaining his creation now that the grass is up and luscious. 'It's all yours," he announced."

When it comes to maintenance, intuitives are left unchallenged. In assembling toys, erecting swing sets, putting up drapes and pictures, intuitives are likely to have more imagination than patience and mechanical know-how. They'd rather design a wagon than put one together according to someone else's directions. They'll study a wall and estimate where pictures should hang, which a sensing person is likely to take time to measure. You might find several nail holes behind pictures hung by an intuitive.

As I look back on childhood jobs, I now know why I detested dusting the furniture in that ten-room house with an ornate winding staircase. There was no permanent improvement from my efforts. Besides, it was a lonely job. My only enjoyment was getting the job finished; playing mind games while I worked got me through solitary jobs.

Although I hated to snap beans and shell peas and butterbeans, when I had a partner I could tolerate the repetitious, boring job. Having conversation gave meaning to the time spent. The overall process and challenge of canning fascinated me, and Mother saw to it that each of us was involved. Gathering eggs was fun because of the possibility of discovering new nests in the hay barn. But gathering eggs in a controlled chicken house would have been unbearable. However, having to complete a routine chore with my hands and receiving praise for finished work contributed greatly to my self-esteem. Mother taught us to take pride in work. Being a structured child who enjoyed scratching items off a list certainly aided my toleration for the physical responsibilities of rural living.

Unstructured intuitives have a rough time keeping things in order. Unstructured sensing people *see* what needs to be done and put it off until a big mess motivates them, but unstructured intuitives may not even see the clutter. If it were not for conscientious sensing secretaries, some executives, doctors, ministers, professors, and counselors would be embarrassed by their working environment. They want things clean and neat, but they prefer to depend on others to maintain physical order.

"When my job was doing evening dishes," Jill, an unstructured intuitive, recalled, "my mother used to get furious because I'd begin at 6:00 and not finish until 9:30. I just can't get started on jobs I don't enjoy. In fact, anything I don't like to do is work. Anything I like to do is play. I'll play all night, but give me work, and I'll go to bed at 8:30. If it's considered a job, basically, I don't like it." Yet, what Jill considers play—writing a term paper, doing research, or solving emotional problems—a sensing person is likely to regard as an unpleasant task.

Intuitive children will spend more time planning how to get out of physical work than it would take to do the job. Adult intuitives take great satisfaction in working themselves out of jobs.

"I'm not very popular at work," Rhonda admitted, "because my co-workers think I'm trying to make them look lazy just because I'm always driving myself to improve over yesterday's quota."

"Everyday I have to increase the number of sandwiches I make in a minute," Jerry said. "I despise working in a fast-food restaurant, so I have to set up some personal goal. The other kids hate me for working so fast, though."

If intuitives have a boring, unchallenging job, they need to insure that after-work activities are geared to learning and improvement. They can do repetitious physical jobs so long as there's design or variety involved.

Knowing that an intuitive's hungry mind is not that person's own creation should help sensing parents and employers to appreciate the special needs for variety and challenge. Teachers' awareness could transform school experiences for many bored-to-death intuitive children.

Naturally, all intuitives have to do physical work, just as all sensing persons are periodically obliged to consult the idea world. But being aware of which process one favors will explain why opposite endeavors are draining. This understanding is certain to ease tension in families where intuitive children—or spouses—are regarded as lazy because they don't like physical jobs. The parents' challenge is to instill in children the stamina needed to discipline themselves to do what they do not enjoy.

Variety—The Spice of Life

Intuitives like to kill two birds with one stone: talk on the phone while cooking a meal, filing cards, or doing exercises. "I consider driving a complete waste of time," Carolyn said, "unless I can be involved in a challenging conversation or listening to a worthwhile tape. Otherwise, I'd rather push a button and instantly be at my destination."

Intuitives need variety because once they learn to do something, they are ready for a new challenge. Repeating an action or filling an order or stacking products does little to satisfy them. Many feel guilty for quitting or changing jobs or losing interest; they scold themselves for being undisciplined. But unless a job or assignment has meaning and challenge, intuitives have to make an effort to complete it.

As an intuitive, I really like doing some sensing things, such as washing windows, cooking, or sewing. However, I rarely cook the same dish twice or use the same pattern in sewing. Jim laughs when I ask, "Did you notice anything different about the oatmeal this morning?"

Intuitives love the complex. They'll make a complicated ordeal out of a simple little task just to get their minds involved.

"Although I am a skilled hydraulic mechanic," Walter remarked, "and I can fix anything on an automobile, I am bored to death with fiddling around with routine maintenance on my own car. Those things I hire someone else to do."

Battling Arrogance

"Oh, I just love to learn" or "Isn't learning fun?" are remarks of intuitives that tend to intimidate or threaten those who are not so directed.

Intuitives are natural teachers and instructors. However, they may elect to begin in the lower grades and progress with the students, stretching and reaching new goals. Elementary intuitive teachers are likely to become bored after they learn the ropes. "If it were not for the fellowship of teachers at middle school," Janeen sighed, "I'd die from boredom." Many intuitive teachers eventually migrate to the college or adult education level.

Sensing mates frequently become frustrated because intuitives never seem to settle down and be satisfied with what they know. "I thought Margaret was just putting on an act," Stan admitted. "I thought she was acting educated or intellectual to impress others. Now I know different."

"Arrogant? I'm not arrogant!" Ryan declared. "When you say that what your wife has to say isn't important, isn't that being arrogant?" I challenged. "That's not arrogant," he defended. "That's true! Arrogance to me is assuming that I'm more important." Barb doesn't want to encourage Ryan in any way since in her opinion he's already too overconfident.

But the reason for reaction is easily explained. Intuitives are amazed when no one else on a committee suggests the possibilities and solutions that appear easily and instantly to their mental computers. They may be amazed and surprised and possibly even frightened by the depth of their perception. It may be easy for intuitives to assume that they are wiser than sensing people, but when they discover that God has specially gifted intuitives with the ability to project and encircle situations, it is inappropriate to presume superiority. The feelings of superiority and inferiority are exactly the same, except one is naked and the other is clothed—neither attitude is adult or pleasing to God.

People who possess a love for learning and respect for new ideas often repel those who are no longer consciously pursuing learning. "I'll never read another thing," one woman declared, "because I don't want to learn anything else. I know all I want to know."

In personal relationships, sensing people who appreciate as God-given their own abilities and those of intuitives will not engage in competition or put-downs.

Because intuitives prefer reasoning over repetitious experiences, they may have a difficult time relating to small children. Spouses often express grave concern over an intuitive mate's obvious disinterest toward their children, but are relieved to discover that it is normal and that attention will improve and increase as the children mature.

Intuitive Decisions

In making decisions, intuitives engage special abilities related to the anticipated outcome. In fact, intuitives are likely to say, "Since it happened that way, in no way will it occur again if I have anything to do with it."

Intuitives dream toward the result desired, then set in motion those things that will insure the projections will materialize. Intuitives tend to think up programs and then depend on sensing people who are well equipped to maintain, mend, build, or run them.

Intuitives sometimes lose sight of their dependence on sensing people and become overly confident of their ideas and ability to manipulate or direct others. Extroverted, structured intuitives especially tend to give overbearing directions to others. "Our children hate to walk through the kitchen on Saturday mornings," Margo recalled, "because of the lists of jobs their father left. He even makes lists for me, which I greatly resent." Structured, intuitive parents can see the overall design of work completed if everyone contributes.

Intuitives need to be reminded of their limitations. Trying to decide who is the more important—the idea person or the worker—is like trying to determine who has the greater input into creating a child. When individuals are aware that all they are or can do comes from God, no one has room to boast.

Spiritual Vision

Because spiritual matters are often abstract—based on personal growth in attitude, human relationships, future possibilities, and probabilities—many intuitives are drawn toward the ministry. Yet, some sensing parishioners become disenchanted with a minister who cannot tighten screws in the bannister and change light bulbs in the restrooms.

Intuitive church members want a minister who will preach brilliant sermons and inspire them to greater spiritual growth. Sensing church members want a minister with these qualities, but also one who doesn't mind getting his or her hands dirty and can administer church finances.

This vision-oriented attitude carries over into one's intercessory prayer life. Intuitives can visualize what they desire for a particular person or group and pray to that end. Intuitives readily relate to Hebrews 11:1, 3 and 12:1-2:

> Now faith is the assurance of things hoped for, the conviction of things not seen. . . . By faith we understand that the worlds were prepared by the word of God, so that what is seen was made from things that are not visible. . . .
>
> Therefore, since we are surrounded by so great a cloud of witnesses, let us also lay aside every weight and the sin that clings so closely, and let us run with perseverance the race that is set before us, looking to Jesus the pioneer and perfecter of our faith, who for the sake of the joy that was set before him endured the cross, disregarding its shame, and has taken his seat at the right hand of the throne of God.

The organized church needs both visionaries and those who will keep the homefront stabilized. Since 75 percent of the world is sensing, congregations will be predominately service-oriented. The difference in type shows up on workday at the church. Intuitives prefer to be on the building, outreach, or future strategy committees. Cutting weeds, laying sidewalks, and repainting the fellowship hall will attract only the very spiritually committed intuitives, while sensing people are drawn to it by the very nature of the physical project. They will particularly enjoy decorating the tables and deciding on menus and the style of serving, while intuitives would much rather engage the speaker and plan the program.

Knowing the unique strengths and preferences of parishioners does away with disapproval and misunderstanding and makes it possible to carry out a church's programs efficiently and effectively, with good rapport as an extra bonus.

Family-Unit Vision

Because intuitives live for tomorrow, they can project which habits will set negative or positive precedents for their children. This may explain why intuitive parents prefer to be in charge of their children. Their intent is to inspire their children to be the best persons they can be and to discover and use their talents to the fullest advantage. By discovering their children's type, parents can adjust unreal expectations and release their young to become their own true selves and to pursue fulfilling vocations.

Dreaming ahead, as intuitives do, adds an element of expectation and excitement and gives a family unified direction, while facing the reality of today is the unique contribution of a sensing parent. How fortunate are those children who have one of each!

Marriage Vision

Since intuitives can sense relationship problems long before they surface, fortunate is the marriage where the intuitive has confidence enough to mention and discuss these insights and exercise problem-solving ability.

Both parties are frustrated, and arguments result when a sensing person's straight-line fact-gathering is pitted against an intuitive's circular style of drawing ideas out of thin air. A sensing mate needs to understand that an intuitive does not omit facts to deceive, but rather considers many facts too unimportant to mention. In this situation compromise will be possible.

Conversation

Intuitives are usually brimming with questions, so their resources for maintaining conversation are endless. However, introverted intuitives may not have confidence to initiate dialogue. Because they tend to be introspective and deeply involved in thought, they may come across as aloof and hard to know. On the other hand, extroverted intuitives can initiate conversation and draw information from a complete stranger.

By God's design, intuitive minds can swish around five or six unrelated items simultaneously, while sensing people are wired for one or two concentrated ideas. Knowing this relieves a lot of marital and family conflict.

Give sensing people factual accounts, and they finish sentences and endeavor to give notice when someone changes subjects. Because their minds go full speed, intuitives mentally fill in lulls in conversation.

"Who are you talking about?" Roland asked impatiently. "Mrs. Nicholas," Sue snapped. "When did we mention her?" "Oh, after we discussed Jennifer, I was thinking about all the people she asked for help and remembered how much Mrs. Nicholas reached out to her. I guess my mind just kept going silently."

Intuitives don't realize how disconnected their statements sound to sensing people who are genuinely interested but often confused. An intuitive backed into a verbal or physical corner may react with possibility-thinking. "I rebel," a spontaneous intuitive explained. "I don't run; neither do I fight physically. I just think of ways to outsmart my attacker." Sometimes this verbal ability to wiggle out of a tight spot is considered manipulative. Often the strategic weapon is stony silence. A structured intuitive—an even-keeled, problem-solver—will attempt to reason things out patiently with an assailant.

Speaking

Intuitives are usually skilled speakers. "We are our own audience and have to be excited about what we say," an intuitive executive explained. "We have to find what we say new and refreshing."

When recalling an experience or telling a joke, intuitives are likely to vary the story so much that someone hearing the second rendition may question the new facts or omission of certain details. Common complaints are: "You didn't tell me that part" and "You've changed your story."

First, carbon copy recitations bore intuitives. Second, intuitives often personalize their accounts to include specific facts and ideas with which the current audience can identify. These embellishments are not lies—just adjustments for the sake of the audience.

Writing and Counseling

Many intuitives are drawn to writing, whether it be personal letters, journals, short stories, research, or observations. They also record so they won't forget. ("My brains are on paper," one intuitive admitted.) Such persons are attracted to psychiatry and clinical and counseling psychology, helping people to understand themselves and others and solving relationship problems.

Money Matters

Although logical-thinking intuitives can understand complex mathematical calculations, most of them prefer not to take care of mundane finance. Writing down or keeping track of figures is so boring to intuitives that most have discovered the less they have to do with money, the happier they are. "Learning numbers and studying financial reports has been one of the hardest things connected with business," an executive confessed.

Conclusion

Spotting the intuitive bicyclists is easy because they zigzag down various paths. Personalized jackets and hats also identify them. Their baskets contain books to read in case of delay, binoculars, notebooks for recording discoveries and ideas, and bags for unusual finds. An intuitive riding with a sensing companion needs to slow down because sensing cyclists carry water, lunch, repair kits, and bug spray.

Heavenly Father, help me to avoid waste by being observant and checking all the facts before making decisions. Help me, too, to channel my efforts in one direction.

Notes

[1]Isabel Briggs Myers and Peter B. Myers, *Gifts Differing* (Palo Alto CA: Consulting Psychologists Press, 1980) 178.

[2]Keirsey and Marilyn Bates, *Please Understand Me* (Del Mar CA: Prometheus Nemesis Books, 1978) 102-103.

Chapter 7

Logical Deciding—
All Head

Do not seek your own advantage, but that of the other.
—1 Corinthians 10:24

We will now examine the contrasting ways in which people make decisions. This variety, too, is God's design. Hundreds of men and women with whom I have talked verify that their decisions are not necessarily based on their sex, environment, or childhood background as they had supposed.

The majority of females are comfortable letting emotions dictate in making decisions, while the majority of men are inclined to base their decisions on intellectual (logical) considerations. Deciding by emotions is more people-directed; logic is primarily situation-based. Interestingly, God has wisely mixed up the sexes on decision making, entrusting a sizable minority of men (four out of ten) with a tender, emotional temperament, and equipping a considerable segment of women (again, four out of ten) with the more impersonal logical approach.

Fortunately, these exceptions to the rule undermine society's tendency to stereotype males and females and releases individuals to be as God created them. We can also see that parents are not to take the full blame for unexplained inability, refusal, or reluctance of their offspring to adopt the parental patterns for traditional male/female roles—independent/dependent, masculine/feminine, strong/weak.

For a man to discover that he is tenderhearted or a woman that she is coldhearted can be a disturbing, yet helpful, revelation toward self-acceptance. Understanding that these traits are God-designed allows individuals to identify their true preference and to strengthen the weaker side of their nature.

Profile of a Logical Decider

When someone discovers that their way of dealing with people and situations is God's idea, healthy self-esteem can emerge, and this in turn improves marriage and family relationships and communication in general. When persons have self-esteem, they will guard against allowing oversensitive emotions to rule totally or allowing impersonal logic to alienate. Some people know immediately what their inclination is; others must struggle to find out. Answering the following questions will help you determine your natural preference.

❑ Are you often regarded as cold, inconsiderate, stubborn, selfish, impatient, unforgiving, or all business?

❑ Do you rarely admit you are wrong without irrefutable facts to prove it?

❑ Are your decisions based on cause and effect?

❑ Do you prefer to make situation-based decisions, considering what seems to be the fairest, most practical, economical, or efficient rather than how you or anyone else feels?

❑ Can you tolerate others disagreeing with you?

❑ Are you rarely moved to tears?

❑ Are you able to discourage hurt feelings and guilt from lingering on your mind?

❑ Can only those people who mean a lot to you hurt your feelings?

❑ Are you more concerned about making the right decisions than about avoiding hurting feelings or disappointing people?

❑ Can you tolerate someone getting mad at you?

❑ Do you make your decisions without apologies or explanations?

❑ Do you generally stick with decisions once you make them, even though people you respect disagree with you?

❑ Do you get impatient with repeated mistakes?

❑ Would you consider firing someone who wasn't doing his or her job to be relatively routine?

❑ Are you comfortable going places or doing things alone?

❑ Are meeting standards and filling needs enough to satisfy you?

❑ Can you function without hearing verbal "thank yous"?

If you answered yes to most of these questions, you probably are a logical decider.

Though all of us use both logic and emotional feeling in decision making, we trust one method over the other. If you are pretty sure you decide first and feel second, you are probably a logical decider and should have little difficulty with the world—if you are male—since that is considered normal.

Females who prefer to make impersonal cause-and-effect decisions, however, are not as readily accepted or understood either by men or women. They often intimidate warmhearted men and women, thereby drawing much criticism for their strong stands. Even the most logically minded females seem to have a dose of emotional judgment, just as emotionally sensitive males appear to have a slight tendency toward logical decision making. All of this is by God's design.

People who decide by logic, though appreciated and admired because they keep our world steady and strong, often are misunderstood and criticized for their lack of expressed emotion. Spouses and children feel very secure and safe with thinking-by-logic parents, yet often chafe under their impersonal analysis and attitudes.

Understanding and appreciating these traits require some effort but promise great dividends.

Appreciating Logical Deciders

Logical deciders prefer to make situation-based decisions rather than people-based decisions. "I just think about the thing I'm going to do and not about others who are involved." Such a statement is fairly typical of logical deciders. Considering the people on the sidelines involves a little extra effort, which logical thinkers are willing to give only if they are reminded.

When sensitive mates, children, or co-workers realize that logical thinkers are endeavoring to make the best use of their money, time, and resources and are not trying to benefit personally, their firm manner can be appreciated.

"If a decision pleases me, I'm satisfied," Sam explained, "even if others disapprove. That's the way it is! Give me enough facts to show me that my decision is inferior, and I'll change it. But just being agreeable isn't my style."

Many mates and children assume that a head-logic partner or parent makes cold decisions out of spite or to show who is in charge. But by God's design, half of all people are more comfortable making those impersonal cause-and-effect decisions. Our world would be in dire straits were it not for people who are capable of making hard-nosed, situation-based decisions.

Understanding that our national security and social stability depend on those who lead with their heads toward goals that require firm, straight-to-the-point transactions should give us a fresh appreciation for the unique, strong contributions of logical-deciding men and women.

In order to carry out heavy responsibilities, to avoid and correct mistakes, those in authority must be tough and decisive and stick with decisions. For this reason, many logical deciders are accused of being unreasonable or stubborn. "I'm not stubborn, just right," they defend.

Employers who make situation-based decisions want to get the job done in the most efficient way. Therefore, they feel obligated to eliminate or reassign workers. Working closely with people and being aware of their needs, abilities, moods, and feelings just slow a logical person's production. "If you don't like it, you can lump it," many say curtly.

"Could you fire your own mother?" I asked a manager. "I sure could," he said without hesitation. "But I would never hire her in the first place because I wouldn't want to fire her."

Those preferring head logic generally don't elect to ask others for their opinions before making a decision. They just consider the known facts and draw the most practical conclusions. Until they are shown limitations in their facts or flaws in their ideas, they're most likely to stick to their decisions. However, the wisest and most practical decisions are not always made on the basis of cause and effect. In many cases, involvement or consideration of people makes more long-range sense than doing the level-headed thing.

Logical deciders are suspicious of those who put emotional argument or pressure on them. They do not like to be manipulated or told what to do. Many of them can take orders, however; but before they comply with a request, they will want plenty of practical reasons.

It is next to impossible to talk logical persons into doing something they do not see any need for doing. Only very strong persons or heavy influence from several colleagues can overrule their reasoning.

The best system I've found to persuade Jim, who is a logical decider, to consider my emotional reasons for doing something is to present him with a neatly typewritten list of his head-logical reasons along with my heartfelt ones and give him time to evaluate the possibilities. If you press a logical thinker for a decision prematurely, especially a facts-and-figures (sensing) person, it will probably be "no." Give the person time to think, and it is more likely to be affirmative.

"The rest of the world isn't paying my bills, so I don't care how they feel about my decisions," Philip announced. "There's only one logical way to act. Who would question it?"

People who decide by logic don't consider others when they have a decision to make because they go from cause to effect and cannot understand why anyone would question such a rational decision. Logical people intend to make "right" decisions no matter how they or anyone else feels.

The majority of deciding-by-logic people are steady and responsible. They believe in an honest day's work for an honest day's pay, and they usually keep their word.

When two head-logic people marry, competition in making decisions is inevitable, and theirs may be a very strict and cold household. Deciding-by-logic parents usually leave little room for mistakes. "I told you once, and that's it—no reminders." Often their discipline lacks warmth and understanding, until they learn from experience the vital part that patience and tenderness play in cultivating relationships with children.

Those who base their decisions on logic may become impatient with the softhearted, people-oriented types. Logical thinkers may indeed speak the truth, but not necessarily tenderly. They do not gift-wrap their statements.

People who rely on logic are usually in charge. They trust their own judgment above another's. Some decisions are never pleasant, but logical deciders seem able to say no more easily and consistently than feeling deciders.

Thinking-by-logic men do not need to proclaim, "I'm head of my home" or "I'm a man." They never doubt it, so they don't rehearse it. Wives of thinking-by-logic men usually feel secure because they know they will have support in a crisis. Thinking men love to hear statements such as: "I feel so protected and safe" and "I trust your judgment."

When a feeling-decider man marries a logical-decider woman, that can present a lopsided problem. "I just can't stand to see my husband dilly-dally around with decisions," Emily declared. "He says he's the man of the house, but he acts more like a scared ten-year-old. I make rules for the kids, which he allows them to break while I'm at work. We fight more over my insecurity with him than anything else. I'm tired of making decisions! I want to lean on him." There can be a solution to this problem, as we shall see later.

Since logical people lead with their heads instead of their hearts, they suffer less from guilt and hurt feelings. Only those special people very close to them are able to hurt their feelings or create guilt. This natural security helps to buffer them against low self-esteem caused by feelings of inadequacy.

The self-esteem of thinking-by-logic men is often threatened by loss of employment or serious illness. Sometimes, if they can no longer provide for their families and offer security, they may assume their trust level and reason for being have been destroyed.

Appreciation of thinking-by-logic persons for specific contributions is an important consideration in building relationships. These people may not advertise their qualities, but they certainly deserve to be recognized.

People who use cold logic seem to have a difficult time saying, "I was wrong" or "I'm sorry." They prefer to say, "You're right" or even "Maybe I'm wrong." They honestly have a tough time agreeing that they really *are* wrong.

People who make decisions through impersonal logic do have feelings, and often deep feelings, but they are equipped to think through hurts and put-downs.

"I don't have time to be hurt," John sighed. "I've got work to do!" This characteristic keeps logical deciders away from depression. They know how to weigh the facts. If what someone says isn't true or factual, a logical thinker can forget or ignore it.

"Naturally, it bothers me," Jim will admit when someone has said some untrue or unkind thing about him, "but I can live with it. I know how it really was. That's all that matters."

The goal of logical deciders is not harmony, but to get the job done. "Hurt or disappoint as few people as possible, but don't let people stand in the way of doing what needs to be done," Randy advised. "If they don't like how you're doing things, let them bail out before they get hurt."

Logical deciders want others to like them, but their self-esteem does not depend on popularity. They respect their own logic and adjust their actions to be agreeable up to a point. However, they would rather be right than popular; but they'd like to be both.

Giving others verbal appreciation is one of the toughest assignments for those who make situation-based decisions. Many wives complain that their logical husbands never compliment them. Since logical thinkers are accustomed to doing what needs to be done with or without praise, they assume all people can function that way. Wives who function better with attention and approval are wise to inform their logical husbands of such need. Generally, thinking spouses will respond positively, but they may need reminders from time to time.

Fathers and mothers who prefer logical thinking need to train themselves to give adequate appreciation and affirmation to their children. Too often they notice only those actions or responses that are not up to standards. Children who decide by logic will not need as much verbal bolstering, but everyone needs a certain amount of praise and recognition.

Unless logical deciders learn to appreciate adequately the importance of others' feelings, they may become authoritarian, stern, and unapproachable. This attitude often alienates them from family and friends.

Introverted logical deciders who are characteristically sober, serious, and quiet, without realizing it may be particularly intimidating to sensitive, sympathetic people. When introverted logical deciders discover that friends and family are not comfortable around them, many become alarmed and upset. Beneath all that seriousness lies a measure of softness and concern waiting for some unthreatened person to draw it out.

Children who prefer the logical decision-making process are likely to intimidate or embarrass parents. I recall how upset I became with our ten-year-old Roger because he refused to play with a guest's son his own age. No amount of sideline cajoling altered his conduct. Fortunately, our older, more sympathetic son David came to the rescue. Later, I reprimanded Roger severely for being unkind and selfish. I told him I was ashamed of him and very disappointed. How differently I would deal with that situation today. Roger was not acting that way on purpose. That was his real self: a logical thinker, insensitive to the other little boy's feelings.

Today, with an additional ten years' maturity and training, Roger is an exceptionally warm and considerate host. Yet, his logical thinking comes through loud and clear in his resistance to outside manipulation.

A mother who is an emotional decider is not only intimidated, but also suffers from guilt because her 12-year-old daughter seems completely callous to the feelings of others. "Where did she learn this?" "Where have I gone wrong?" asks the mother. Now that she understands God has gifted Pam with logical decision making, the mother has relaxed. Pam isn't a finished product yet. Patience, prayer, and understanding will help her become balanced.

When thinking-by-logic persons are accepted and exposed to a steady diet of warmhearted and considerate decisions where people express their disappointments and feelings kindly, they more easily learn to consult the emotional-deciding process they possess.

Often logical deciders reared in strong, emotional homes become quite proficient in using their sensitive side. That's why it is surprising when questionnaires on emotional decisions indicate that some soft-acting people really prefer the thinking decision-making process. In such cases, home background and environment have been influential.

All in all, logical deciders can display caring and consideration, but they are like rocks or bricks that must be warmed up periodically.

Conclusion

The thinking-by-logic bikers lead the pack. They flush out any wild animals, remove fallen trees or rocks in the path, and decide on detours. However, they are apt to ride so far ahead that they are unaware when one of their bikemates falls behind or has trouble. Once they see the need, however, they will respond with sound logic, warmth, and tenderness. We really do need to appreciate and encourage our thinking-by-logic men, women, and children.

Lord, help me to be aware of other people's feelings and needs, and help me to consider humbly the opinions of others.

Chapter 8

> # Emotional Deciding— All Heart

Love your neighbor as yourself.
—Matthew 22:39

In everything do to others as you would have them do to you.
—Matthew 7:12

The second pattern of decision making is based on values and emotions and is attributed chiefly to women. When men show sensitivity, women may be attracted to their warmth and friendliness. Yet they are often considered weaklings by those who actually depend on them. Women are not criticized for being softhearted and sentimental, but men are often restricted from openly expressing their feelings.

All people have feelings. Logical thinkers, the so-called hardhearted people, *do* suffer from rejection and criticism. Emotional decision-makers are more influenced by other peoples' needs and opinions.

After you ascertain that you make decisions based on emotions and values, you can learn to cope with this fact and get the best mileage from God's special gift to you. Answering the following questions will help you discover your inborn preference.

❑ Are you warmhearted?
❑ Do people think you are considerate, friendly, unselfish, patient, and forgiving?
❑ Do you make people-based decisions primarily?
❑ Do you prefer to hear another person's opinion or preference before you make decisions?
❑ Do you need harmony?
❑ Do you tend to take the blame just to keep peace?
❑ Do you dislike arguments?
❑ Do you want everyone to like you?

❏ Are you flexible?

❏ Are you likely to change your plans when someone is inconvenienced?

❏ Are you more comfortable as an employee than as a boss?

❏ Would it be difficult for you to fire someone even if you had good reasons?

❏ Are you sensitive?

❏ Are you bothered with hurt feelings and guilt?

❏ Do you often feel inadequate?

❏ Do you easily shed tears at another's misfortune?

❏ Are you tactful?

❏ Do you avoid hurting another's feelings?

❏ Are you apt to ease into the truth rather than say it bluntly?

❏ Do you avoid controversial subjects?

❏ Are you apologetic?

❏ Do you preface many of your sentences with "I hope you don't mind," "I'm sorry to be late," "Would it hurt your feelings if . . ." "Could I bother you . . ." "Please forgive me, but . . .," "I hate to disagree, but . . ."

❏ Do you feel guilty when someone goes to extra trouble for you?

❏ Do you prefer to have a companion when you go places and do things?

❏ Do you like to hear verbal thanks for services rendered?

❏ Do you often feel sorry for yourself because others don't seem to appreciate your hard work?

❏ Do you need approval?

❏ Do you need to hear "I love you" from your spouse and children?

❏ Are you sentimental?

From your affirmative answers you'll know whether or not you are primarily attracted to emotional decision making. Everyone is a blend of both logical and emotional deciding.

Females don't have to apologize for their indecisive and sensitive reactions because this is the accepted or expected attitude. Their struggle comes from allowing others to take advantage of their good nature, from declining to stand up for themselves or to make negative decisions. I talk with mothers who agonize over the disrespectful way their older teenagers treat them. Disrespect seems to attract disrespect. However, men who prefer making emotional decisions seem to have the most awkward and painful adjustment to make. It seems unnatural and unacceptable in our society for men to dislike making difficult or negative decisions and to stick by them or succumb to tears. "I certainly have doubted my manhood," Ralph admitted. "I've been trying to prove to myself and my family all these years that I was head of the house, strong, disciplined, and tough. I may sound like it, but inside I die a thousand deaths."

Just as logical women suffer ridicule, so sensitive men are put down, laughed at, and mistreated. This often drives them to bars or fights or questionable sexual activity.

Just as logical thinkers can learn to consult their emotional decision making, so sensitive people can develop logical, protective decision making, although their preference will never be based entirely on logic.

Appreciating Emotional Deciders

Feeling decision-makers prefer to make value-based decisions that make everyone happy. Even though they consistently experience disagreement over decisions made at home, church, and work, they still strive to make decisions that receive 100% approval from all involved. However, thinkers are quick to remind us that one decision will never satisfy everyone. So, it's not only okay to disagree, but also healthy. Remember that if an emotional decider doesn't object, a thinker assumes agreement—which is often far from the truth.

Feeling types have to learn to respect their opinions as well as their decisions, even when others disagree. If they do, eventually they will be able to tolerate the awkwardness of feeling a bit selfish or mean. Softhearted people must determine not to let anyone push them around, control them, or take advantage of their softheartedness and desire for approval and harmony.

People-Based Decisions

Those who by nature consider people first when making decisions make up 50 percent of the population. Although they make warm, thoughtful, unselfish decisions, their troubles are many.

"I wish you hadn't said anything; now I don't know what to do," said Jean. How a decision will affect others is the concern of people-based decision-makers. Putting people first seems to go along with Jesus' teaching to treat others the way one wants to be treated, but there needs to be balance between pleasing people and doing what makes good sense. The second commandment is "love your neighbor as yourself" (Matt 22:39). The important word here is "as." We're to love others not more, not less, but equally.

"I just want to make other people comfortable," Ralph said. "It hurts me to see handicapped or mistreated people." This deep concern for the physical and emotional welfare of others attracts sensitive people to service-oriented professions. In fact, sensitive persons whose work does not actively touch others may be unhappily employed. If you are an emotional person working away from people, you may want to find other ways to bring people into your life.

Because they lead with their hearts, people who decide by emotion are easily influenced by comments, looks, and situations. However, we don't have to reach a ripe old age to discover that it is impossible to please even one person totally and always.

Sensitive people come across as indecisive because they are so easily influenced by the opinions of others. Consequently, they will never feel 100 percent good about relationships since people keep changing. Knowing this helps sensitive persons accept mixed emotions as normal. Emotional deciders have to learn to deal with bad feelings if they want to make and stick with wise decisions.

It is extremely important to sensitive, emotional people for everyone to like them. "Even the people I can't stand, I'm devastated if they don't like me," Trena shared. Because these people want others to like them, they are likely to make decisions that guarantee popularity but often ignore good sense. This pressure can be eased if these tenderhearted people acknowledge that their world will not end if everyone does not like them. People have such varied tastes that it is unrealistic to assume one can satisfy all.

The Bible urges us to be patient with others, but it doesn't teach us to be doormats in order to be popular. The apostle Paul instructed believers to do their best to get along with people, but he certainly wasn't popular with everyone. Even Jesus was not totally popular.

Emotional deciders fear being selfish. They want others to be happy, no matter the cost to themselves. Emotional deciders need to be cautious about allowing others to take advantage of their good nature.

Though many emotional deciders are in positions of hiring and firing, they find terminating anyone very difficult. For example, when a business-owner friend of mine realized he was emotionally sensitive, he lamented: "Now I understand why I have 160 employees when I only need 130. I just don't have the heart to fire anyone."

This tendency to soothe and understand emphasizes the patience of sensitive persons. Whereas deciders-by-logic may display patience with a machine, deciders-by-emotion are more likely to apply patience to people.

"My mind is telling me right," Clara said, "but I'm just not believing it. I'm always questioning my motives. I'm my worst enemy. I assume people expect me to do what they want, but I have found that people respect me more when I say 'no' when I feel no."

"I feel so bad when my decisions disappoint others," Juanita said. "But if I please them, I displease myself. I'm not sure if I'm doing anyone a favor because I end up resenting the person and disliking myself."

I'm convinced that many prayers of emotional people are confessions for disappointing others or for resentment and angers that result when they deny the right to God-given personal preferences. However, just because sensitive people struggle with mixed emotions and have a tendency to allow others to overrule them, that does not mean they are never selfish or hard to get along with. Quite the contrary. Just as logical deciders, especially those who've encountered the Lord, can often be the kindest, most thoughtful people, embittered emotional deciders in charge of their own feelings can be the ugliest. Although sensitivity comes naturally, make no mistake, thoughtfulness is taught.

Emotional deciders exude warmth and acceptance toward others. When someone is crying, they're likely to join in. Even if people have brought on their own troubles by stupid mistakes and uncurbed appetites, sensitive people reach out to the poor, ill, abused, alcoholic, drug-addicted, ignorant, or depressed. Because they are sympathetic rescuers, hard luck stories really tug at their hearts.

Intuitive emotional people are drawn to those who suffer emotional and relational disorders. With their ability for possibility-thinking, they can encourage the most depressed and discouraged toward spiritual solutions.

Sensing-emotional people are particularly adept at providing for physical needs. However, they need to be careful so that no one will take unfair advantage of their generosity. Talking things over with a logical decider regularly is wise.

I gladly run my decisions through Jim's mind. I don't always agree with his opinions, but I certainly do consider them. His opinions are usually the most protective of me. Because I'm an emotional decider, I have a tendency to work myself into the ground as long as someone is crying for help. But if I listen to Jim, I avoid burnout and wasted effort.

Every emotional decider I've interviewed agrees that harmony is the central desire of their hearts. Since any disagreement threatens this harmony, they are likely to take the blame or not mention their "druthers" just to keep peace. But not saying what's on one's mind just to avoid an argument is a lie. "Better a $4.00 filter today than a $400 repair job in nine months because I was too nice to argue," said Ron, a logical decider.

"When my husband and I disagree," Janeen said, "I usually end up crying, and he gets mad. Just one time," she said cautiously, "I'd like to hurt his feelings—just to prove that he has some. But I give in and do it his way. It's easier that way. Even if he'd consent to do it my way, I'd feel guilty about his disappointment. Can't win for losing."

"I would rather be warm and considerate than right," Rosemary concluded. "I just detest argument and will do anything to avoid it. I can't bear to hear neighbors argue. I want to go settle them down and get them to forgive and to understand each other."

Whereas logical deciders will violate their hearts to make a practical decision, emotional deciders will violate their hearts to keep peace or please someone. Neither way is always best, but care should be taken by sensitive persons to consider practical solutions. When emotional deciders take it on themselves to make allowances or to discount their desires, they unconsciously prevent logical deciders from accommodating others.

Becoming familiar with God's word and allowing the Lord to direct our people involvements gives us not only the most positive and balanced perspective, but also the needed confidence to be consistent.

Emotional deciders are very sensitive to criticism. Because they are likely to assume responsibility for anything going awry, they can hardly handle the situation when their motives are questioned or misunderstood or when they are mistakenly blamed.

Carol nosed her car into the gas pump because the gas tank was on the opposite side of her car. She had been waiting patiently in line for some time. When a stranger yelled at her and scolded her for pulling her car in that way, his remarks upset her so that it ruined her whole day. Emotional people need to be more particular about letting others hurt or intimidate them.

Emotional deciders have a tendency to want others to be as concerned about them as they are about others. This can cause much tension and hurt in a logical/emotional home.

"I get hurt feelings because Rich doesn't tell me anything," Sandy whined. "It hurts me that I find out what's going on from other people. 'Didn't you know about such and such?' or 'Didn't Rich tell you that we did so and so?' my friend will ask. I'd like to think I was important enough to be told these things firsthand," she continued.

"I'd like to speak in my defense," Rich objected. "The reason I don't pass those things on to Sandy is not that I think she's unimportant, but because I don't consider the information important enough to remember. Most of it is just plain garbage anyway."

Because emotional people are interested in hearing minor matters, they view withholding information as a personal affront and put-down. Logical deciders, however, do not collect facts for the purpose of passing them on to others. They store what they hear in their mental reservoirs so that when the opportunity comes, they can pull out the information. To them, the degree to which they share information is not synonymous with the importance they put on a person.

The sensitive spouse who really wants to catch up on details can get them by asking questions. But to assume that information is being withheld purposely will do nothing but cause hurt feelings and destroy trust. On the other hand, when logical deciders become aware of the importance emotional deciders put on being informed about matters involving people, they can discipline themselves to share such news without a cross-examination in the evening.

The logical-thinking husband assumes that he's done his part by providing a good paycheck, a comfortable home, and marital faithfulness. But he feels an added burden when his wife expects him to express his thanks to her for doing what he thinks she ought to do in the first place. He does not expect her to thank him for working, so why should he express verbal appreciation to her?

When logical men and women discover that emotional persons don't function well without verbal acknowledgment, they conclude that developing a considerate attitude is a small price to pay. Sensitive people pick up rejection like magnets, but they are easily encouraged with a few words of appreciation. (My book, *Appreciation—What Every Woman Still Needs*, discusses this dimension.)

The desire for harmony at any cost, guilt over displeased people, and disappointment at not receiving thanks or appreciation threatens the self-esteem of emotional deciders. They cannot respect themselves unless others respect them. This is opposite of the inborn self-respect of logical deciders.

Sensitive people often give out the message, "You can pick on me." When we have a low opinion of ourselves, we are likely to believe whatever anyone says about us, especially if it is uncomplimentary. However, when this tendency is understood, emotional people can learn to think their way toward self-respect by identifying the lies they feed themselves and stopping the condemning process.

Using "I" statements helps feeling-judgment persons to be decisive and quells low self-esteem. For example: "I reject that statement." "I refuse to argue." "I disagree."

Sensitive people often feel their decisions are second class until they gain some confidence. Since emotional deciders by God's design receive the majority of their self-esteem from the positive feedback of others, they are encouraged to reach out and care for people.

Some confusion arises when ministers and counselors assume that women receive most of their self-esteem from their husbands. This is often true, but logical-deciding women who receive a good part of their self-esteem from their careers or from their own sense of sound judgment will not be as emotionally dependent on their husbands. This may threaten the male's security and sense of authority. Conversely, emotional-deciding men, although they will receive esteem from their jobs, especially if the employment directly involves people, will also attempt to extract some self-worth from their wives.

When unemployed sensitive mothers (or fathers, for that matter) experience an empty house, their self-esteem is likely to plummet. Many slip into depression simply because they do not feel needed or appreciated. They do not hear thanks or see an important reason for living when they are not actively contributing to another's welfare every day.

Some women react to this situation by picking on their husbands, indulging in self-pity, or intruding into their adult children's lives. A better way to bring more people into their lives in a positive way is to do volunteer work, find employment, develop new skills, enroll in college, or get involved in church and community activities.

Emotional deciders are naturally more conversational than logical deciders because they need to be with and help people physically and psychologically.

"My husband loves kitchen talk," Lona said proudly. "Not that he's a sissy or anything, but he doesn't seem bored with all my long, drawn-out explanations. He listens to what the children have to say, too, which is more than I can say for my brother! His kids have to defend themselves in one short sentence."

Because they are comfortable around people and need to converse, some introverted-emotional people resemble friendly, outgoing extroverts.

Knowing that a child is an emotional decider will help a parent give him or her fewer solitary jobs. Sometimes a parent assumes a child is lazy when he or she is really lonesome. Parents of sensitive children can also be alert to questionable companions or to those who might be taking advantage of their softhearted, easily persuaded children. A little counsel and encouragement can make children aware of their need to use their heads to protect their hearts.

Dealing with a Softhearted Male

Sensitive little boys may cry often and be picked on because they take everything so personally. This causes most adults, especially mothers and grandmothers, to come to their aid and protection, actions that increase the boys' vulnerability. Mothers and fathers often disagree on how to treat tenderhearted little boys. "Let him stand up for himself; he's got to learn someday," a father will boom. "But he doesn't like to fight, dear, and we don't want him to become a bully, do we?"

Ironically, many of the fighters at school are softhearted fellows trying to win acceptance. Sensitive teens are also apt to be drawn into compromising activities just because they want to be accepted or considered normal. In an effort to protect themselves, many male emotional deciders develop a tough veneer that cannot be penetrated until years later.

Softhearted men are few in number, but their problems are many. Just going over characteristics common to emotional deciders made Bill, a 6'4" mechanic, choke up. "I'm all that," he admitted. "What can I do about it?"

To maintain a dependable balance of security and stability for their wives and children, sensitive men must learn to juggle being sentimental, softhearted, indecisive, and peace-loving with weighty masculine responsibilities. We owe it to them to understand their plight so we can appreciate their struggles and offer encouragement.

"You're so lucky to have a man to live with like Gerald," Emma sighed. "He's so considerate and friendly." "Oh, really?" Bonnie shrugged. "You have no idea what it's like having an indecisive husband and father on your hands. I'd like to know that I could fall apart and he'd be able to pick me up."

Although warmhearted, sensitive men are quite appealing to women, those attractions may turn sour after marriage. Most wives just cannot understand, appreciate, or feel secure with them. Because it is not considered manly to be indecisive, sensitive, and softhearted, many of these men struggle with a feeling of inadequacy, doubting their manhood. Often they cover up their lack of inner confidence by talking and acting tough. Subconsciously, they want to camouflage their tenderness so they won't get pushed around. "No one is going to shove me around," Jerry declared. "I'm a man, and I'm going to stand up like a man." Men who are confident of their manhood do not have to declare it.

Another way men deal with this gift of sensitivity is by withdrawing to protect their feelings. Fortunately, some men channel their energy into vocation, religion, hobbies, or sports, while others negatively depend on alcohol, drugs, gambling, or marital infidelity to give them a sense of strength and manliness.

Softhearted men seem to be attracted to marriage for companionship and want to make life easier and happier for their wives. Logical-deciding men want to exchange financial security for care of home and children.

By God's design, wives want to lean on their husbands to make difficult decisions. But when a wife observes that her husband topples with the weight of decision making, she often reacts with insecurity—which makes him feel more inadequate. In her insecurity the wife may become very bossy and resort to using war-words: should, ought, must, and need. When these authority words are preceded by *you*—you *ought* to do this or that; you *need* to stand up for yourself; you *should* be the head of this house—the husband is put on the defensive. Argument ensues, and often hitting occurs. People are usually very surprised to learn that sensitive men who want harmony and peace are more likely to hit their wives and children out of frustration that all is not well.

When a husband relies on his wife to make the majority of household decisions and expects her to handle most of the discipline of children, he forces her into the parental role while he assumes the passive child role. Marriage is for adults, not parents or children.

"I know I can have anything I want," Elaine said. "Homer would deny me nothing. He gives me my way. He'd spend his last dime on some little thing I want. But I hate him for it. I'd really like for him to say no to me sometimes. I would respect him more."

When a wife realizes that her husband is by God's design especially ten-derhearted, she can assist him by agreeing to bear the weight of responsibility together. In this way she will assist him in learning to consult and develop the logical decision-making process (his less-favored way of making deci-sions) and increase her security at the same time. This is well worth the effort.

Balancing Heart with Head

With practice, softhearted people can learn to use the impersonal, logical decision-making process. When a tough decision is to be made, knowing that the first inclination will be a heart decision, emotional deciders can use discipline to drag it right on to the head. After a brief exposure to questions such as, "Is this fair to me?" "Do I really want to do this, or do I feel like I should do this to avoid feeling guilty?" "Is this the best use of my time and money?" I ask myself, "What would Jim say or do?" Learning to say no or displeasing others is an assignment for emotional deciders, but those options must be exercised when dealing with persons who try to take advantage of them.

Conclusion

The bikes of emotional deciders are equipped with passenger carriers. These sensitive cyclists make sure everyone has a companion and is comfortable and happy. Their baskets are loaded with supplies to share. When someone lags behind or displays a need, they will slow up to keep that person company, even if it means missing out on a side trip. They want to be sure they are wanted and appreciated.

Teach me knowledge and good judgment, for I believe in your commands.

Chapter 9

Work—
It Must Be Done

But all things should be done decently and in order.
—1 Corinthians 14:40

By God's design you are either an information-gatherer or a decision-maker. Although you daily function as both, you will prefer one over the other. You have already determined your preference for one of the two ways of gathering information—by sensing (facts and figures) or by intuition (ideas and possibilities) (chapters 6 and 7). And you have discovered whether your preference is for making decisions based on logical thinking or on emotional feeling (chapters 7 and 8). The process you are most comfortable using with your friends and co-workers will reflect your lifestyle preference, which will be either structured and organized or unstructured and spontaneous.

If you are most comfortable as an information-gatherer—through sensing facts and figures or intuitive ideas and possibilities—you will lean toward the spontaneous or unstructured lifestyle. But if you prefer the decision-making process—using either logic or emotions—you will probably follow the structured lifestyle. Of course, each of us is a neat combination of structure and spontaneity, depending not only on our inborn gift, but also on our background, environment, and other influences.

There's a little twist in what the choice of lifestyle reveals about extroverts and introverts. Extroverts use their favorite process on the world—"what you see is really me!" Extroverts who prefer the decision process will show their structured side to the world. But extroverts who prefer the facts or ideas process will display spontaneity. Extroverts generally engage their second favorite process during their introversion time, which may be very limited.

Introverts, however, use their *least* favored process with their friends and co-workers—"what I bestow is just my shadow." They reserve the use of their preferred process for their private lives. This means that when you confront an introvert who has a structured lifestyle, you are actually seeing his or her second favorite process. Introverts whose favorite process is making decisions, either logical thinking or emotional feeling, will reveal to the world their spontaneous side.

Therefore, extroverts are privileged to use their favorite process most of the time and may depend very little on, or seldom use, their second choice. Introverts rely heavily on their alternate preference and may not develop or use their first preference as much.

Profile of the Structured Lifestyle

We are dealing primarily here with the process we actually use with our friends and co-workers, which clearly determines our lifestyle. For instance, structured persons brought up in an unstructured environment will no doubt adopt a mild bent for the spontaneous way of life. Or an unstructured person exposed to a structured environment will learn to consult structure more, though still preferring the spontaneous lifestyle.

Structured persons reared in a highly organized home will more likely be extremely structured—inflexible, perhaps. However, even if unstructured persons live with structured people, they will still prefer spontaneous reactions. Likewise, structured persons who live among the unstructured will instinctively prefer an organized, structured existence. That's because God created us the way we are. We didn't decide how we wanted to be, although many people spend much of their lifetime trying to change themselves *and* others—all to no avail.

Although our society is primarily structured, spontaneity plays such an integral part that no one has any authority to claim one is superior to the other. However, a healthy respect for each lifestyle pattern and its benefits can contribute significantly to enjoying and adjusting to life and work. It will ease tensions and promote personal and family harmony as well as bubble over in our employment, church, and other relationships.

The differences in lifestyle seem to create much of the friction and disagreement in modern marriages. But when each lifestyle is viewed as God's special gift rather than as a deliberate personal choice taken for the purpose of being hard to get along with, partners can actually have fun comparing and adjusting their lifestyles. According to the Myers psychologist team,

> This preference makes the difference between the judging [structured] people, who order their lives, and the perceptive [spontaneous] people who

just live them. Both attitudes have merit. Either can make a satisfying way of life, if a person can switch temporarily to the opposite attitude when it is really needed.[1]

Most of us operate under both lifestyles, but fit more comfortably with one over the other. Sometimes we may be more structured at work and less so at home, or vice versa.

As you check the descriptions below that apply to you, remember that only you know exactly how you prefer to be. Whether or not you've ever been totally free to develop God's design for yourself is another matter. Some people—especially feeling ones—have lived according to someone else's stipulations for so long that they feel guilty being themselves.

❏ Are you a planner?

❏ Do you prefer to plan your day ahead of time, then adjust if the weather or situation changes?

❏ Do you enjoy making lists in your head or on paper?

❏ Do you have to finish a job or project before you are satisfied?

❏ Are you most likely to finish a job or project before you begin another?

❏ Are you concerned about wasting time?

❏ Are you likely to plan three or four things for the same time slot?

❏ Do you make lists for others?

❏ Do you believe that work earns playtime?

❏ Do you suffer a twinge of guilt if you read a magazine article before the dinner table is cleared?

❏ Are you likely to get many projects finished before you can justify going on vacation?

❏ Do you get some sense of satisfaction even from completing unpleasant jobs?

❏ Do you work better with a deadline?

❏ Are you disciplined to hand in reports on time?

❏ Do you prefer to arrive early for a meeting rather than walk in at the last minute?

❏ Is it relatively easy for you to take instruction from others?

❏ Are you likely to follow prescribed rules without question?

❏ Are you a rule maker?

❏ Do you expect others to follow the rules?

❏ Do you prefer life on an even keel rather than excitement and changes?

❏ Are you more cautious than risk-taking?

❏ Do you consider yourself a homebody?

❏ Do you prefer to know ahead of time "what's going to happen" and "who'll be there"?

❏ Is it natural for you to keep your belongings and papers neatly organized?

❑ Do you usually know where to find things?

❑ Do you enjoy routinely straightening drawers, toolboxes, cupboards, or bookshelves?

❑ Do you prefer to follow an organized procedure?

❑ Do you like to follow a time schedule?

❑ Is your day divided into segments—morning, afternoon, and evening, or even hour-by-hour?

❑ Do you usually want to know what time it is?

❑ Does punching a time clock or being at work at an exact time agree with you?

❑ Do you usually decide on a time to begin and a projected time to end?

❑ Is your lifestyle fairly predictable?

❑ Do you have certain days to do certain chores?

❑ Are you likely to let someone know you are coming for a visit?

❑ Do you prefer knowing plans ahead of time?

❑ Are you likely to be bothered by last-minute changes in plans?

❑ Do you enjoy attending meetings?

❑ Do you usually plan to arrive on time and stay for the entire meeting?

❑ Do you enjoy having appointments and the security of knowing you have certain places to be at certain times?

❑ Do you rarely forget an appointment?

If you checked most of the boxes, you probably prefer the structured lifestyle over the unstructured and spontaneous. Now that you know God gifted you with the structured lifestyle preference, you will understand how you can sometimes make others uncomfortable and why others sometimes arouse your impatience.

Appreciating the Structured Lifestyle

As a structured person, you should be able to credit God's gifting for most of your self-discipline and organization. You should also be released from any unnecessary rigidity and find it easier to relax your high expectations of others. By the same token, when unstructured people understand what motivates you, they will gain a new appreciation for the constant pressure under which you work.

A year after members of one family had discovered one another's preferences, one of the female cousins commented, "Have you noticed how everyone seems to be nicer this year?" Individuals were automatically making allowances for the different ways they knew the others were operating by

God's design. Structured people can even clash with other structured people, so understanding and appreciating this lifestyle can ease much tension.

Planning and Scheduling

Making plans gives security to structured persons. They prefer to live in a planned, decided, orderly way whereby they can regulate life and control it. Their plans are like invisible pegs over which their day is stretched. Once they've planned something, they intend to follow through, like the woman who balanced her umbrella while she finished mowing the lawn in a downpour—an extreme example. Unstructured people prefer to wait until they see what kind of day it is before they decide what they'll do. Consequently, they have fewer changes in plans.

Structured people project not only what they'll do tomorrow, but also what they'll do next week and next month. Some can't go to sleep unless they know what they'll prepare for breakfast and what they'll wear to work. Unstructured people often resent the regulated, looking-ahead lives of the structured. To them, it's a sure way to ruin a good day and a good time. But to structured persons, an unplanned day is a wasted day—and wasting time is as dreaded as disease.

The last thing many structured people do before falling off to sleep is recall all they accomplished that day and think about what's on tap for tomorrow. "I like to know what I have to look forward to," Les said. Structured people feel insecure if they don't know what's ahead.

Organized people prefer to set a time to leave on a trip, then squeeze in what needs to be done—while spontaneous people prefer to leave when they get ready.

"I want to leave on vacation—any trip—at 6 AM," Dick said. "My wife is never ready to leave before 10:00. So we compromise by leaving at 8:00. It takes me two hours to help her get her chores finished," he continued. "Really, she'd rather leave on a trip at 11:00 the night before," he chuckled. "I could look at it as before 6 AM couldn't I? That way, we'd both win!"

"My husband is even structured when it comes to lovemaking," Martha complained. "He has it set in his mind a certain day, an exact time. Kind of ruins the spontaneity for me," she mused.

"Joe likes surprises," Mary said. "I like to know a week ahead if we're going out on Friday night and where," she continued. "Joe says that spoils his fun, and he prefers to wait and see what comes up before he commits his evening."

Compromising between these two preferences will require little adjustment. Mary wants to know on Monday, but perhaps Joe could bend his preference a bit and let her know on Wednesday. That would give her some time to look forward to the evening. Occasionally, he could allow things to be completely planned ahead; occasionally, she could be totally flexible. Both attitudes are good for the soul. Structured people need to be careful about scheduling someone else's life.

Making Lists

To make sure their day will fit their plans, structured people rely on lists so they know exactly what needs to be done and they won't forget anything. "If I lose my list," Wanda remarked, "I might as well go back to bed."

Some structured people merely form lists in their minds, while others designate even the exact time they will begin a certain chore. While spontaneous people regard lists as restrictive, structured people gain freedom and security from them.

Structured individuals take satisfaction in scratching items off their lists. "I even write things on my list that I know I won't forget—like eating lunch," Carolyn quipped, "just so I can strike them off."

"The reason I make a list," Ralph commented, "is just to clear my mind. Otherwise, I'm trying to remember everything I have to do. When I write it down, it's like clearing my calculator. I may not even have to look at the list."

Even the very young structured make lists, especially around Christmastime. Structured children respond positively to lists, while unstructured children resent them.

I have always credited my mother with my appreciation for the organized way of life because she raised us on daily lists of jobs. Actually, she just appealed to what was already present in kernel form. (She had only one unstructured child, and as I recall, lists had little effect on him; nor was he ever in a hurry to complete his chores.) Completing those lists of tasks contributed significantly to my self-discipline and self-esteem. Behind every listed job is potential praise.

Structured people should be careful not to let a list take priority over common sense, however. They will do themselves a favor and reduce tension among friends and family if they will just refer to their lists rather than obey them rigidly.

The plans and lists of structured persons merely facilitate doing what they prize the most—getting finished. They are driven to finish tasks. Even in the tasks they love doing, finishing them produces the major satisfaction. Projects do not necessarily have to be finished today. They can be started again on schedule and continued as long as the task requires.

If structured persons dislike a chore, they will finish just to begin jobs they enjoy doing. They are more interested in the ends than in the means. "I rush projects even when I enjoy them," Ronald admitted. "I tell myself to slow down and enjoy this, but before I know it I'm sweating like a horse just to get it finished."

Structured people regard anything that gets done as work—and they like work. Work is always more important than play. In fact, they do not allow themselves playtime unless their work is finished. This is not always virtuous because God also created humans with a capacity and need for recreation and play. Extremely structured people never get all their work done, so they may lead a very "un-fun" life, and may also restrict their children. Structured mothers remind, "The dishes must be done before you ride bikes," or "Get your toys picked up before you watch TV." "Work earns play time" is their code of ethics.

"I can't knit with a clear conscience until my work is done," Thelma confessed. Knitting is regarded as play. Structured feeling people have to fight guilt when they play before work is finished.

Structured people have difficulty sitting down in a cluttered house even to read the Bible. They feel compelled to straighten every rug and paper before they begin. Spontaneous people read whenever they feel like it and for however long they are interested.

To the structured types, the ultimate luxury is having an entire day to work at finishing chores. Then they can justify all that time "wasted" on more pleasant things. Structured people need to learn to unwind. This they can do by putting recreation and social time—like they schedule dentist appointments—on their precise calendars.

Locked to the Clock

Even when structured persons are interested in a project at hand, the clock can stop it. The interest of spontaneous persons, on the other hand, doesn't quit until the process no longer interests them—even if it lasts 36 straight hours.

Structured people probably ask, "What time is it?" more than those who are spontaneous. Most organized people don't eat when they get hungry, but when the clock indicates it's time for a meal.

"The clock puts me to bed, and the clock gets me up," Amy announced proudly. "In fact, I sleep with my watch on—I want the dial to glow all night." In my counseling experience I've discovered that many spontaneous people don't even like to wear watches, whereas structured people have the time posted everywhere.

The typical day of structured persons is frequently divided into neat little segments; they know what time it is without looking. Their day is more like a big lollipop, which they lick until it's gone.

One of the hardest things for structured persons to do is lie in bed in the morning after they are fully awake. They think: "I ought to get up and get started," "I'll never get my work done if I waste time on my back," or "Make hay while the sun shines." A spontaneous lady said, "I have no trouble lying in bed wide awake if there's nothing exciting to get up for."

Deadline-Oriented

Structured people respond well to deadlines. In fact, deadlines serve as their encouragers. Deadlines are dreaded by the spontaneous—"It's like iron hanging over my head," Sue said.

Appointments made ahead are like little hooks that hold a structured person's day together. To spontaneous folk, however, appointments resemble hostile bosses.

Sometimes structured people are so appointment-oriented that they don't know what to do with a lull in schedule. Structure then becomes a security blanket to protect them from idleness.

Organized

Structured people usually enjoy keeping drawers, closets, and possessions orderly. Because of their respect for deadlines and for doing things in order, organized people generally enjoy setting and enforcing rules. By rule keeping, they can avoid unnecessary crises. "My structured mother panicked when she opened the last can of baby's formula last night," Jessica said. "She prefers to have enough on the shelf for a national disaster."

Organized people are happier if nothing happens that is not planned; that is why they are *not* the best persons in crises. They can handle crises when they have to, but they definitely do not enjoy that kind of responsibility. In such situations structured persons would be fortunate to have a spontaneous person to lean on.

Conclusion

The kind of friction that can develop in a structured/spontaneous home is obvious. Compromise is the only solution because there's no way a structured person can become unconcerned about the time or a spontaneous person can be transformed into a clock-watcher. Structured people can learn to loosen up on the time and allow spontaneous people to share their more casual approach to life.

Just knowing that some people plan their lives while others let theirs unfold will help people see the need for compromise. Each gives a little without expecting the other to change completely. Isn't it funny that we are attracted to our opposites, yet endeavor to change what we were attracted to? Compromise can be fun—like little puzzles to figure out—but compromise depends on the open, honest communication that springs from people who have healthy self-esteem.

The structured bicyclists have arrived quite a while before the scheduled departure time. Their bikes are lined up in perfect symmetry, and the baskets are neatly packed with supplies. They nervously check their watches, comparing them with others'. They study the itinerary and rules sheet, marking the points of interest that appeal to them most.

Thank you for the discipline you've given me, Lord. Help me to be flexible and not let the clock rule me. Give me patience with those who are less organized.

Note

[1]Isabel Briggs Myers and Peter B. Myers, *Gifts Differing* (Palo Alto CA: Consulting Psychologists Press, 1980) 9.

Chapter 10

Work—
It Must Be Fun

So do not worry about tomorrow, for tomorrow will bring
worries of its own. Today's trouble is enough for today.
—Matthew 6:34

Our world runs primarily on structured tracks, and most people consider being structured, self-disciplined, and organized the mature way to be. But a closer look at what a sizable proportion of people enjoy doing and how they spend their money reveals that the spontaneous lifestyle is alive and well respected.

Although great emphasis is placed on production, employment, financial success, and work-related goals, labor contracts are brimming with demands for shorter working hours, increased personal leave days, longer vacations, better working conditions, and the like. A brief scan of checkbooks, closets, and recreation rooms will indicate that people believe in play and recreation.

Advertisements tout products and services for use on the beach, lakes, and ski slopes and at parties, sports events, and plush vacation spots. Our nation has even moved official holidays to Mondays to provide longer weekends. So time off from work for play and rest from organized life is in vogue. Home conveniences, computers, cordless phones, appliances, and so forth are all geared to making work more fun and life easier.

Profile of the Spontaneous Lifestyle

The fact that half the world is work-oriented and the other half is play-oriented shows God's wisdom in designing a seesaw with perfect balance. But maintaining this balance is not possible without a careful analysis of the legitimate spontaneous segment.

To determine if you prefer the spontaneous lifestyle, in the boxes below, check the characteristics that apply to you.

❑ Do you prefer to let your day unfold rather than plan the events?

❑ Do you prefer to wait to see what the weather is like before you make plans?

❑ Is it more important to enjoy what you are doing than just to get it finished?

❑ Do you enjoy the process of a project or job more than completing a list?

❑ Are you relatively unconcerned about time?

❑ Do you rarely consider the time involved in an unplanned conversation, doing something you enjoy, or playing a game?

❑ Do you dislike alarm-clock awakenings?

❑ Does punching a time clock repel you?

❑ Do you regard the day as one unit rather than individual hours or small segments?

❑ If you don't enjoy doing something, is it like "pulling teeth" to make yourself do it?

❑ Do you regard doing anything you dislike as work?

❑ Are you prone to do what you enjoy first rather than tackle jobs you are obligated to complete?

❑ Do you let things slide before beginning a project?

❑ Do you have many unfinished projects?

❑ Do you strongly dislike deadlines?

❑ Do you dislike someone looking over your shoulder and telling you what to do?

❑ Does following prescribed rules irritate you?

❑ Do you consider rules primarily for troublemakers?

❑ Do action and excitement motivate you?

❑ Do you find yourself strangely drawn to emergency situations?

❑ Are you unusually calm in emergencies?

❑ Do you consider yourself unorganized?

❑ Do you often misplace your keys, checkbook, glasses, etc.?

❑ Do you dislike straightening and arranging your belongings, stacking wood, filing papers, etc.?

❑ Do you often have to improvise because you failed to prepare thoroughly?

❑ Are you likely to forget time or fatigue once you get started on a project you really enjoy?

❑ Are you fairly competitive?

❑ Do you prefer events to be exciting and unpredictable?

❑ Do you like to decide at the last minute rather than plan exactly what you are going to do?

❑ Do you prefer the outdoors where you can be free from the confines of four walls?

❑ Do oceans, rivers, mountains, etc. hold a special attraction for you?

❑ Do you like to feel free to go and come as you like rather than be tied down to a system?

❏ Do most meetings bore you?

❏ Does the idea of making appointments turn you off?

❏ Do you dislike making appointments because something else more fun might come up?

❏ Do appointments hang like iron over your head or give you the feeling of being handcuffed?

If you checked most of the preceding boxes, you are no doubt more spontaneous than structured. There is no need to apologize for being unstructured because society hungers for comedy relief and the antics of those who are comfortable with surprises and crises. So, if you're spontaneous, get ready for mental release that you're okay. You just have to work harder to complete jobs and be on time.

Appreciating the Spontaneous Lifestyle

Everyone wants to be structured, it seems, because they believe it's superior. Even spontaneous people are likely to think so.

"I've spent all my life watching structured people operating systematically and trying to be like them," Jill sighed, "but it's been impossible. I've just made myself miserable all these years trying to be someone I'm not," she continued. "How released I feel now that I know God made me and half of the world spontaneous individuals. I feel as free as a young colt in the springtime. Let's go get a pizza and celebrate!"

Understanding and accepting one's temperament is a giant step toward developing self-esteem. And since spontaneity goes against the grain of our structured society, learning to appreciate the process is half the battle. Many strong, wise, perceptive people are unstructured. Our world is certainly indebted to them. They are fun to get to know.

Let the Day Unfold

Spontaneous people want to understand life and adjust to it rather than organize and control it as do structured people. They live for the moment, enjoying every sunrise, flower, and breeze; fluctuating with the rise and fall of the events of the day.

God designed half of us to prefer that our day unfold naturally. Unfortunately, these people are often unappreciated and put down; called shiftless and lazy; and scolded for being unorganized and late, loving to play, forgetting things, and failing to plan ahead.

Spontaneous people would rather wake up slowly and glide into the day. "I just want my day to unravel," Bernie signed. But because our world is structured and runs by the clock, the majority of unstructured people are awakened by noisy alarm clocks. Unless they have an exciting day ahead, they reluctantly drag out of bed.

Spontaneous people resist making plans ahead of time because the weather, people, and situations are so unpredictable. "If you look forward to an event, you risk being disappointed if it rains or something," Allison explained. "If you just do it, there's no disappointment—just fun." To spontaneous persons, looking ahead to events is not as exciting as participating in them. They prefer to make decisions each day: "Shall we go to work?" "Shall we go fishing?"

"My boyfriend has fun on his mind all the time," Anne complained. "Why, he carries his fishing pole and football in the trunk of his car—always ready for sports. He says work is just a terrible interruption to a day's activities."

"I don't like to put too many restrictions on my day," Ed said. "I'd rather take things as they come. No pressure that way."

Structured people feel that taking things as they come exposes them to more pressure. But spontaneous people are gifted with handling the given moment with expertise, using whatever resources are at hand. Spontaneous people rarely say, "I'll take the toolbox just in case," because they don't expect problems to develop.

"Sometimes I wish I were spontaneous," John said, "because I get tired of thinking and planning all the time." However, spontaneous people *are* always thinking because they are operating from scratch for most situations.

Spontaneous people generally don't like to weave their lives around a schedule, but prefer to weave their schedule around their lives. "Watching the time worries me," Ted said, "so I threw my watch away."

"I have to hear the last whistle blow before I get started," Leland said. "But I have no problem leaving work at the first squawk of the whistle."

Spontaneous people will let time get away from them doing what they enjoy, then at the end they steam out a two-hour job in an hour and a half.

Because spontaneous persons operate out of excitement and action, it may take them half a day to start the day. But they are likely to keep the day alive long after structured people have zipped their eyelids shut.

"I come alive after 10 PM," Larry said. "My favorite time is from 10 until 2 AM. No meals to bother with or ordinary things to bog you down—pure freedom."

"If I have too much time, I spin my wheels," Gilbert said. "The more I have to do, the more I get done. That's why I let the garage pile up until my wife threatens to divorce me if I don't clean it. I like to see a great big improvement when I'm finished."

Spontaneous people don't do things ahead of schedule because that would ruin the fun, excitement, and action of the challenge of limited time.

"I would rather play and save just enough time to get the job done," Amanda said, "than have too much empty time on the tail end."

Since spontaneous people need excitement and action to motivate them, they have their own ways of creating a crisis around routine jobs.

"I let my room pile up for a month," Janice said. "Then I take a shovel and begin," she laughed. "I'd rather have a mammoth job to accomplish than a rinky-dink 30-minute bother. When I was a teenager my mother took a picture of my cluttered room and proceeded to show it, not only to my friends, but also to their parents, hoping that would shame me into making my bed and keeping my clothes hung up," she continued. "Well, it didn't work. I was mortified and very angry," she said bitterly. "I still resent her intruding on my privacy. I'm 33, and my room is still a mess," she shrugged. "I'll clean it when I get time."

Once spontaneous workers get started on assignments they enjoy, they lose track of time. If I ever have to undergo a critical operation, I want a spontaneous surgeon who doesn't care if he or she misses lunch or meets his or her schedule!

When things pile up on spontaneous persons, they roll up their sleeves and plow in. Conversely, when structured persons face heavy pressure, they feel inclined to hide.

Process-Motivated

As long as spontaneous people enjoy the process, they don't care what time it is, what meal they've missed, or that they are dog-tired. Merely finishing things does not give unstructured types the same sense of satisfaction as the structured. Spontaneous people work on inspiration. When they are free to choose the time and method, the job will be done better and quicker. By the same token, when given a responsibility that lacks challenge, unstructured persons can piddle around with a two-hour job all day.

"If I'm in the process of doing something, and the phone or a visitor interrupts me, I lose momentum completely and may never return to my job," Lillian admitted.

"Lying out in the sun is not just to get a tan," Rachel explained. "I really enjoy the whole process."

"When I've got a plumbing job that I enjoy," Robert shared, "I almost hate to finish it. In fact, I drag it out a little bit," he grinned.

An onlooker may admire the discipline of a spontaneous person involved in an action-packed project, but that person is probably more fascinated than disciplined. Finishing something is not the goal, but rather enjoying the process.

Spontaneous people who are serious musicians and athletes practice, not out of discipline, but because they enjoy it. They practice until they are weary, not until the timer goes off. Spontaneous types may often take more time than the structured want to give to practice. When they are sufficiently challenged by the action, spontaneous contestants easily run off with the majority of competitive prizes.

Starters

Spontaneous people prefer to start things and let others finish them. Consequently, many structured people receive credit for the ideas of spontaneous people. Great designers and artists are often spontaneous starters, and the most profound thinking and writing no doubt emanate from introverted intuitives. Brilliant teaching and speaking are done most frequently by unstructured extroverted intuitives, because their structure doesn't interrupt or stop their ideas and experiments. The world oscillates on the unstructureds' inexhaustible sources of unique ideas, but usually they depend on structured people to put them to good use.

Taking care of business as usual—the tedium of a job—presents little challenge to spontaneous persons; they want to get something going. "When everything seems to be moving smoothly," Carl signed, "one of those restless guys has to stir the pot." Spontaneous intuitives are often those "restless" ones.

When a spontaneous person who designed construction equipment realized that foreign purchasers were unable to follow the English operating instructions, he took it on himself to study Spanish so he could put the operations manual in their language. Now that's an innovative, challenging task!

Unstructured intuitives are likely to have three, five, or more projects going at the same time, which bothers their structured mates and family. Their spouses are likely to refer to these partially finished pursuits as failures, time-wasters, or messes.

"I haven't lived long enough to finish anything," a man in his 30s declared. These ideas in motion often cause criticism and argument, which destroy trust as well as self-esteem, to say nothing of the stress created in marriages.

Spontaneous people, knowing that their strength is in starting rather than finishing, can curb this tendency for impulsive decisions by forcing themselves to consider all the facts and the wisdom of investing time and money in the new project. When they understand that their motivation is short-lived in certain areas, and unless they have a mate who is willing to fill in the gaps or keep the challenge alive and fresh, they will be wise to exercise more discretion. Learning to focus will alleviate problems.

"If it's work, basically I don't like it. Anything that's work isn't fun. Anything fun isn't work, in my estimation," Jill quipped.

"The way I handle one of Mom's after-school lists is by doing the jobs I like best, then playing awhile. Right before Mom comes home I do the things I don't like to do—real fast."

Many activities that spontaneous people regard as fun—for example, translating operations manuals into Spanish, painting skyscrapers, fighting fires, rebuilding engines, working out on the track, composing music, landscaping a yard, running a camp, operating heavy equipment, and rescuing people—structured people categorize as work. In fact, to structured persons, everything they do is work; otherwise they consider it wasted time. Make work seem like fun, and spontaneous people will enjoy doing it.

Most unstructured intuitives heartily agree that there is one huge, constant routine-responsibility that is completely void of fun: housework. "I've tried it. I don't like it. So why punish myself doing it?" one spontaneous single reasoned. "I seldom make my bed, except when I change it," Geraldine chirped. "Who sees it?" Most unstructured persons prefer outside jobs where they sense more freedom, freshness, and excitement.

"If I could just tear into one disastrous, wrecked room," Janell explained, "I sure would enjoy it. But this daily dusting, straightening, arranging pillows, sweeping floors is for the birds! I've gotta see great improvement before I enjoy cleaning," she continued. "Just let me know someone is coming, and I really get motivated to clean up the house. I might even wash the windows!" she mused.

"I never do housework in the daytime," Jennie said. "I just can't see wasting good sunshine and daylight on something so boring. I do most of my cleaning after 9:30 at night. I enjoy putting up drapes, planting flowers, working in the garden, baking, writing, or painting the picnic table. But those things aren't work; they're fun. In fact, anything I don't *have* to do isn't work," she added, "even if it's scrubbing floors for someone!"

Spontaneous Sue assumes no one likes to do housework since she doesn't. "Because I'm the wife and mother, I feel it's my responsibility to do it," she lamented. "But when I put off clearing the table to read the paper, my husband, Pete, who is structured, commences to clear it. This makes me feel guilty because I think he's not only doing my work, but also doing a distasteful job." Pete says he enjoys helping around the house, so Sue is feeling unnecessary tension. "It's one way I can show her how much I love her since I'm not a talker," he said.

"My daughter-in-law is driving my son crazy," Erma said. "After visiting them for a week I understand how he feels. I knew she was very lackadaisical about keeping up the housework, but can you believe that she saves dishes for days before she washes them? She sticks them everywhere. I told her that it's easier to do a few dishes everyday and always have her kitchen looking half decent, but she says she'd rather face a colossal disaster area one day than be tied to tiny boring jobs all week."

Because housework or any routine task isn't much fun for spontaneous people, they get little satisfaction from merely completing jobs. If they plan to hire someone to do anything, it should be those jobs.

Some organized people consider the unstructured's dislike of tedium as an excuse for what they don't want to do and label anyone who is late, disorganized, or forgetful as lacking in self-discipline.

Structured people often take for granted their built-in self-discipline toward work. The subtle satisfaction they receive when a job is finished motivates them to do their cleaning chores first thing in the morning. Structured people need to understand that anytime an unstructured person accomplishes anything considered work—uninteresting or routine—it requires great self-discipline.

This, unfortunately, does not rule out the possibility for laziness and lack of discipline. We all get the lazies, but structured people are better equipped to fight the lack of self-discipline because of their drive to finish things. Unstructured folks have to work harder to find ways to spruce up work. Lack of finances certainly forces unstructured people to do many things they dislike doing. There are ways, however, to make unpleasant jobs more enjoyable; for example, listening to tapes, doing just a few chores each day, choosing a time that does not conflict with fun, getting the entire family involved. Learning to do what we need to do is part of maturation and life.

Spontaneous Occupations

Love of action, excitement, and risk drives spontaneous people to occupations that reflect their temperament. When unstructured people are bored with their employment, they sometimes blame it on personal inadequacy. But since routine responsibilities without variety are bound to bore them after a while, they blame their unhappiness on their inability to relate to people or assume they are incompetent.

Accepting a boring position is easier when you know why it disagrees with you. Spontaneous persons seem to have a more difficult time finding occupations that suit them, but when they seriously look for a job that involves risk, action, freedom, and excitement, it can usually be located or created.

Spontaneous people seem suited to short-term projects, to meet crises, and then move on to another problem. For this reason, unstructured people are skilled at doing things such as pulling businesses and people out of financial, relational, and emotional crises. They are good rescuers—paramedics, paratroopers, counselors, and emergency personnel. They do their best thinking under pressure.

Spontaneous sensing people seem to like repetition with variety. Spontaneous intuitives are often attracted to occupations such as acting, crisis counseling, or writing. One spontaneous intuitive friend is building robots and designing computer games. At 21 years of age he has already found his niche.

Unstructured people resist doing things that require long, drawn-out discipline, so completing college or graduate work is quite a feat for them.

Those who've researched personality types in depth report that if what spontaneous persons want lies beyond high school or college, they will structure themselves long enough to get the education and training. If they do become teachers, they are usually the favorite ones because their classes are fun and full of variety. Their lack of organization and planning might bother some structured students, but a good mixture of temperament type in teachers is beneficial.

Spontaneous parishioners are often afraid that the church will make demands on them or that they will have to sit in meetings. Unless an activity really excites them, they don't like to commit themselves. Although the spontaneous types carry a significant portion of the teaching load in most churches, the weekly responsibility is forbidding because they're not sure what might surface. However, they might enjoy the process of operating the sound booth, conducting a bus ministry, or pushing wheelchairs—something exciting and different. Structured people don't mind volunteering for nursery work on schedule, but spontaneous volunteers would rather be on an emergency or substitute list and not tied to a certain Sunday.

Similarly, spontaneous people get bored when worship services proceed the same week after week. Intuitives can handle the same routine if the content is exciting. Yet unstructured people often share with me that they think they should *not* be bored in church. "I feel I'm not as good or holy as those people who attend consistently and who look and act all together," Alvin confessed.

Deadlines

"You're late," Joe's boss scolded, as Joe punched his time card. "Better late than never!" Joe retorted. "I don't get paid for the time I'm late, anyway, so why the bother?"

"If I want to leave on a trip at 7:00 AM," Stacy said, "I tell Bob that we must leave at 6:00. Then, I can be pretty sure that we won't leave much later than 7:30. He hardly begins to get ready by the time I want to leave."

To spontaneous persons, deadlines are threats. Therefore, they need lots of latitude in schedule. Deadlines are the signal to get started.

Authority

Spontaneous people don't mind doing what is right; they just resist someone's telling them to do it. *Should, ought, must,* and *need*—war words—will not extract the best behavior from a spontaneous person.

"I can't stand for Mother to tell me to put the cap on the toothpaste, shut the dishwasher door, or turn the lights out," Jed said, "even though I know I should."

"You had better be mighty nice if you tell me what to do!" Janet cautioned.

"I want to be under his wing," George said, "but I don't want anyone to tell me what to do."

A hint to structured people dealing with or directing spontaneous people: Don't tell them when to begin a job or how to do it; just tell them when you want it completed.

Emergencies and Crises

When things fall apart, spontaneous types come alive, while the structured cringe.

"Some boy cut his eye on a door frame," Gloria said. "While the other teachers fell apart, I sent a student to the restroom for wet paper towels and began to administer first-aid. Then a fire broke out—we all smelled smoke. While other teachers got hyper about it, mostly running to see the fire, another fumbled for the fire department's number while I grabbed the fire extinguisher and put the fire out. I was cool and calm through the whole ordeal. It was a neat day!" she said with a smile.

The love for meeting crises often attracts spontaneous men and women to the ministry, missionary work, or chaplaincy. However, handling the routine part of church life—ordering literature, repeating ritual, attending meetings—is likely to get old and be difficult for the unstructured. This is the area where they need fervent prayer support and understanding from their parishioners. Unstructured ministers are likely to become bored after a congregation has gotten on its feet. They may not realize why they have suddenly lost their zeal, but it is because they need to move to another crises. On the other hand, structured ministers prefer to deal with ordinary situations that require long-term shepherding.

This description adequately describes the spontaneous types in top form. A little risk keeps them alert. Just let the fire whistle blow and spontaneous people are raring to go. They would rather just make it to a meeting than sit for even a few minutes with nothing to do.

When I was in high school I wanted to walk to school with my brother, Mac. I preferred to leave early so I could visit my locker, greet friends, and look over notes for the first class. He liked to walk in on the bell. Because he is free-spirited, no one pushed him, not even his slightly older sister. In order to walk with him, I had to violate my structure, but not to walk with him denied my need for companionship. Compromise solved the problem. I walked to school alone, in good time, but took a more casual walk home after school with Mac.

Disorganization

Spontaneous persons may see a time when they have to be structured, and they can be structured for a while without feeling obligated to stay that way. Organized doesn't mean self-controlled, though it often appears that way to others. Unstructured people often feel intimidated or inadequate around structured people.

One young wife complained to her mother, "Bill's mother has no set time for meals. She cleans any old day, but never very soon. She lets pans pile sky high before she tackles the job. But she can sew all day long, and the dust and clutter can be waist high, and she will just continue."

Being structured and organized occasionally makes spontaneous persons feel good about themselves, but they hate the thought of being that way very long. By nature spontaneous persons are not organized, but self-discipline can help them be somewhat that way. It's difficult to get used to the opposite lifestyle, though each has its merits. An attitude of superiority is never justified for either lifestyle.

"I was spontaneous like my daughter," Mrs. Wilson said. "I've just gotten structured since I've grown old." Although we can all remember how flexible and spontaneous we were as children, those who are spontaneous by preference remain that way as adults. However, responsibilities often tend to coerce them into a structured lifestyle. Spontaneous people need to treat themselves to an unstructured day whenever they can.

Free-Spirited

Spontaneous people do not like to feel boxed in. They resist control of any sort. When they get ready, they go!

Spontaneous children of structured parents experience mental and physical restriction. Because their likes and opinions differ from those of their parents, they learn to distrust their instinctive persuasion and replace it with guilt or anger.

A 30-year-old, college-educated woman shared that she was reared in a sect where all girls were required to do indoor chores. Because she was spontaneous, she wanted to follow her father out to the fields, ride the hay wagon, and work with animals. Instead she was relegated to kitchen work, food preparation, and sewing. She was told what to wear, how to think, and how to fix her hair. She was convinced that her total disgust for housework and her desire for independence were due to this restricted background. How relieved she was to discover that God gifted her with the action-excitement temperament. She still has to structure herself to do her work, but she frequently allows herself to be unstructured without apologies.

Back spontaneous people into a physical or verbal corner and they will respond by fighting or fleeing. Intuitives are more likely to resist physical violence, but pushed enough, even they will resort to fisti-cuffs. When a mate becomes too possessive, a spontaneous spouse will back away. In an effort to protect their independent spirit, spontaneous people will sometimes avoid forming intimate friendships or getting heavily involved in an organization. Once they've been manipulated, they subconsciously ward off any claim on them or their time.

Introverted spontaneous people are fiercely independent. Often these people do not like to talk and also dislike being touched. Love is expressed in unique, subtle little gifts such as smiles, assistance, and quiet presence. On the other hand, extroverted spontaneous people love the process of conversation and generously lavish their friends and family with gifts, humor, and services.

When spontaneous people's free-spirited temperaments are understood, accepted, and appreciated, they become less resistant to getting in line.

Structured people can learn from spontaneous people. They would probably suffer fewer backaches and high blood pressure if they followed the example of spontaneous people. "Why worry when you can play?" a released spontaneous person quipped.

Spontaneous Homemakers and Parents

Spontaneous, feeling people—male or female—seem to suffer more than any other type. Because their emotional judgment is sensitive to criticism, and because they are eager to be liked, to please people, to be agreeable, and to be easy to get along with, they encounter many barriers.

Spontaneous women see that their houses are not clean and neat, but try as they may, they never can compete with organized homemakers. Chores such as baking, doing laundry, mending, and cooking are just too boring to do regularly; these they register as more faults in their self-analysis.

One of my unstructured friends has become organized, now that she understands why she dislikes housework. Her whole family is amazed with her orderly life. Her self-esteem has risen 100 percent since she quit bad-mouthing herself for not being like her mother and sister-in-law and the models on TV commercials who dust and wax floors all the time. She doesn't feel guilty when she prefers to let things slide, now that she knows half the people in the nation agree with her method.

Because spontaneous mothers assume they are supposed to be serious about life, they can't understand why they feel like playing and being out of doors. Making and keeping appointments for themselves is hard enough, let alone being responsible for their children's appointments, afterschool lessons, and school activities. When their children's illnesses keep them isolated, they struggle with irritability.

Trying to teach children discipline and to help them form good habits is much more difficult for spontaneous parents. They are likely to be criticized by friends and family for not putting their children to bed at a certain time and not getting them up for school early enough to eat breakfast. (Males who share the same difficulty in finishing boring, routine jobs disappoint their wives, bosses, and family and find that their feelings of inadequacy are magnified.)

One spontaneous wife and mother, who had been reared in a structured home and married a highly structured man, had succeeded in repressing her natural spontaneity to the point that she resembled a fairly structured person. However, when her children gained a little independence, the release of responsibility was more than she could handle; it completely upset her emotional stability and self-esteem. She had been keeping it a big dark secret that she despised all the things mothers are supposed to love to do. But once she had less pressure to do them, it was more difficult for her to make herself continue. Her feelings of inadequacy stemmed from her lack of organization, resentment for being tied down, and her husband's ability to work circles around her. One night she finally confessed her unhappiness and bitter spirit, and suddenly her self-worth began to germinate. Today she is enjoying her spontaneous gift mixed with a bit of guilt and smugness.

School and the Spontaneous Pupil

School is primarily designed for structured teachers and pupils. Spontaneous children tire of projects long before they are complete. They yearn to be outside playing football and and running through the grass. For them, study halls are atrocious additions to the curriculum.

These children create reasons to be excused so they can prowl the halls or find something exciting to do. They are always volunteering to run messages to the office. Sometimes spontaneous children create a crisis just to wake up everyone. If their teacher says, "no whispering" or "no chewing gum or eating candy," their resistance to authority is activated and offers brief challenges for which they often get punished.

When spontaneous children say that school is a drag, they are right! When their teachers declare that all learning is not exciting, they, too, are right; but that acknowledgment doesn't reach spontaneous children. Some learning has to be made exciting and active for the other half.

The same is true for classes at church—children, youth, and adult. If structured people would just learn to trust the spontaneous crowd with crisis situations, our world might be in better shape. Often the structured judge the reliability of someone by their organization and self-discipline so that their God-given potential is completely overlooked. What a shame to waste this special talent!

Conclusion

The spontaneous bikers show up at departure time, still cleaning the sleep out of their eyes. While a few who can be seen in the distance make their way to the starting point, challenges of "Let's race!" can be heard from those who are waiting impatiently. Their baskets carry only breakfast doughnuts and coffee. Their bicycles are equipped with heavy-duty tires and mud flaps because they intend to explore little-traveled paths.

Father, help me to accept the necessary structured part of life with patience and understanding. Help me to develop discipline to finish the things I start and make the best use of the precious time you give me.

Chapter 11

Uniquely Yours

O LORD, you have searched me and known me. . . . Such knowledge is too wonderful for me. . . . I praise you, for I am fearfully and wonderfully made.

—Psalm 139:1, 6a, 14a

Understanding how God designed us and appreciating God's particular choices for each of us greatly increases our self-worth. Being a good original rather than a poor copy provides a positive outlook on life.

By now, you should have your preferences well in mind. Write the letters of your favorite processes:

❏ **E** Extroversion   ❏ **I** Introversion

❏ **S** Sensing/Facts   ❏ **N** Intuition/Ideas

❏ **T** Logical Deciding (Thinking)   ❏ **F** Emotional Deciding

❏ **J*** Structured/Organized   ❏ **P*** Spontaneous/Unstructured
    (Information-based)   (Decision-based)

[*The letters J and P for the structured/organized and spontaneous/ unstructured processes respectively do not correspond to the descriptive words because in my opinion using *Judgment* and *Perception* is somewhat confusing and hampers clear understanding. But in order to utilize the excellent Myers-Briggs Temperament table, we must use their identification key.]

Characteristics Frequently Associated with Each Type

Sensing Types

Introverts / Sensing (IS)

ISFJ–Servers

private and/or quiet, want provable facts/hands-on experience, resist radical changes, lead with heart logic, seek approval, need harmony, want acceptance, organized, work to the finish, respect and follow rules, take or give orders

Extroverts / Sensing (ES)

ESFJ–Host and Hostesses

open, outgoing, want provable facts/hands-on experience, resist radical changes, use heart logic, seek approval, promote harmony, want acceptance, organized, work to the finish, respect and follow rules, take or give orders

ISFP–Sympathizers

private and/or quiet, want provable facts/hands-on experience, resist radical changes, lead with heart logic, seek approval, need harmony, want acceptance, impulsive, play is the process, respect but bend rules, dislike giving or taking orders

ESFP–Performers

open and outgoing, want provable facts/hands-on experience, resist radical changes, use heart logic, seek approval, promote harmony, want acceptance, impulsive, play is the process, respect but bend rules, dislike giving or taking orders

ISTJ–Conscientious Workers

private and/or quiet, want provable facts/hands-on experience, resist radical changes, rely on head logic, expect approval, want trust and/or respect, organized, work to the finish, respect and follow rules, take or give orders

ESTJ–Organizers

open, outgoing, confident, want provable facts/hands-on experience, resist radical changes, rely on head logic, expect approval, want trust and/or respect, organized, work to the finish, respect and follow rules, take or give orders

ISTP–Ustoppable Operators

private and/or quiet, want provable facts/hands-on experience, resist radical changes, rely on head logic, expect approval, want trust and/or respect, impulsive, play is the process, respect but bend rules, dislike giving or taking orders

ESFJ–Rescuers

TP ESTP

open and/or outgoing, want provable facts/hands-on experience, resist radical changes, rely on head logic, expect approval, want trust and/or respect, impulsive, play is the process, respect but bend rules, dislike giving or taking orders

Characteristics Frequently Associated with Each Type

Introverts / Intuituion (IN)

INFJ–Empathizers

private and/or quiet, see possibilities, trust vibes, battle boredom, pursue challenges, set goals, use heart logic, seek approval, promote harmony, want acceptance, structured, work to the finish, question but follow rules, take orders/prefer to delegate

Extroverts / Intuituion (EN)

ENFJ–Encouragers

outgoing, bubbly, assertive, see possibilities, trust hunches, analyze behavior, 10-track mind, battle boredom, pursue challenges and/or goals, lead with heart logic, seek approval, encourage harmony, want acceptance, structured, work to the finish, question and adjust rules, follow orders, delegate

INFP–Idealist

private and/or quiet, see possibilities, trust vibes, battle boredom, pursue challenges, analyze behavior, handle emotional crises, use heart logic, seek approval, promote harmony, want acceptance, play is the process, unscheduled, impulsive, question and bend rules, dislike being in charge

ENFP–Catalysts

outgoing, bubbly, assertive, see possibilities, trust hunches, analyze behavior, battle boredom, pursue challenges, /emotional crises, use heart logic, seek approval, encourage harmony, play is the process, impulsive, question and massage rules, crave freedom and action

INTJ–Expert Strategists

private and/or quiet, see possibilities and reasons, battle boredom, pursue challenges, analyze systems, set long-range goals, rely on head logic, expect approval, want trust and/or respect, structured, work to the finish, question rules, establish own procedure, delegate if necessary

ENTJ–Head Chiefs

outgoing, assertive, confident, see possibilities, trust reasons, analyze systems and behavior, battle boredom, pursue challenges, set long-range goals, rely on head logic, expect approval, want trust and/or respect, structured, work to the finish, question rules, establish own procedure, assume they are in charge

INTP–Think Tank Experts

private and/or quiet, see possibilities and reasons, battle boredom, pursue challenges, handle systems' crises, rely on head logic, expect approval, want trust and/or respect, play is the process, unscheduled, impulsive, brainstormers, resist control, crave freedom, prefer not to be in charge

ENTP–Powerful People Movers

outgoing, assertive, confident, see possibilities, trust reasons, analyze systems and behavior, battle boredom, pursue challenges, handle systems' crises, rely on head logic, expect approval, want trust and/or respect, play is the process, impulsive, crave freedom and action

Jim and Ruth Ward, *Coaching Kids: Practical Tips for Effective Communication* (Macon GA: Smyth & Helwys, 1999) 98-102.

The thumbnail sketch that corresponds to your letters should sound wonderful to you. If it does not satisfactorily describe you, read the other sketches. The one that appeals most to you is probably the closest to your blend.

I've never heard anyone say that they wished to be another type. In fact, I have heard comments more like the following: "What a feather in my cap!" "Too bad the whole world's not like me." "I'm finally who I thought I really was."

No one is forced to behave according to his or her type, but those who violate their favorite preferences for very long are likely to develop problems with themselves or others. The indicator shows potential rather than what one is actually experiencing. Some people admit that they have been ashamed to be different from others in their family or group, so they have completely ignored their inner instincts.

If you want to double-check your type, The Myers-Briggs questionnaire is available through most psychologists, psychiatrists, and counselors. Many businesses and institutions, along with the military, use the Myers-Briggs Type Indicator for placement and for solving personnel problems. Many colleges also include this instrument with other entrance tests for career assistance and personal understanding. A private interpretation is well worth the cost.

"I don't like to be put into a mold," you may argue. But temperament typing doesn't put you into a mold; it merely reveals your pattern in God's design and releases you to be yourself. In the words of Gordon Lawrence,

> An understanding of type frees you several ways. It gives you confidence in your own direction of development—the areas in which you can become excellent with most ease and pleasure. It can also reduce the guilt many people feel at not being able to do everything in life equally well.[1]

Even though your particular type may be one of the more common blends, there's still so much variety within a type because of background and development of individual processes that you won't lose your uniqueness.

Some of the best fun you can have is to compare notes with someone of like type. You'll think you are meeting a long-lost friend because of the similarities. Knowing others in the world who think and decide like you do is very encouraging and comforting.

"When I came for this interpretation, I was really down," Joan said. "But just to know there are people in the world enough like me to warrant a duplicated sheet gives me tremendous confidence."

Distinguishing which process you are using at a given time will help you get acquainted with yourself. Instead of trying to hide your differences, you will become so comfortable with the benefits of your own preferences that you'll be free to develop your favorite processes fully, as Isabel Briggs Myers points out in *Gifts Differing*.

You will also become aware of your less-favored processes and can learn to develop them a little more. My purpose in writing this book is to encourage you to depend on God to help you strengthen and consult your less-used processes and to increase your self-esteem. Myers affirms:

> Learning to use your less-liked processes when they are needed is worth all the effort it takes. They not only contribute to a better solution of the present problem, but also prepare you to handle subsequent problems with more skill.[2]

Because some types are very rare, you may not often meet another just like yourself. For instance, introverted intuitives number only 1 percent of the population because of their double minority preferences. The percentage sinks even lower when males are emotional decision-makers or females are logical deciders. Extroverted sensing people are the most common since both fall into the majority of the population.

"I feel better than I have ever felt in my life," Ann wrote. "It's a wonderful feeling to feel good about myself and to understand myself. It makes it easier for the Lord to use me to help others."

Once we understand ourselves, then we are ready to get acquainted with others and allow their opposite preferences to balance our less-favored processes.

"You can't resent someone for being like God made him, can you?" Elaine surmised after she realized she had been holding her husband's differences against him.

When family members are knowledgeable about one another's preferences, tensions are replaced with forgiveness and admiration. Different situations call for a particular process. For instance, spontaneous people love to plan parties, but the structured are better at carrying out details and cleaning up afterward.

Some of the tensions in a family stem from the structured members attempting to put the spontaneous ones on a schedule and the spontaneous members trying to remove the structured ones from their schedules. Spontaneous people prefer to react and adjust, whereas the structured like to plan ahead.

For years there were things about me that I didn't understand or like, but try as I might, I couldn't change them—not even with prayer. My sister Jane and I had been physically separated for years, but an unusual situation arose that allowed us to visit for a week in our mother's home. I was astounded—and relieved—to see that she thought, talked, and acted almost like a carbon copy of myself. "Why fight it?" I reasoned. "These are deeply engrained family characteristics that I'll never be able to dump." However, I admired and approved of my sister Jane so much that if she were this way, I was content to remain the same. I have discovered since then that our likenesses are due to God's design of like temperaments.

Both Jane and I are ENFJs, which explains why we think, plan, talk, and respond in much the same way. We can almost read each other's minds. It was such fun to visit Jane's home several years later and see that she handles children, company, and emergencies almost exactly like I do.

The following profiles will help you pinpoint your main characteristics and contrast them with other types. The brief sketches have been gleaned from personal interviews with individual types embracing various educational, social, and emotional lifestyles from the following extremes:

- 12-year-olds to 80-year-olds
- High school dropouts to Ph.D's
- Laborers to professionals
- Pew-warmers to seminary professors
- Never-married to triple-timers
- Easily depressed to chronically optimistic
- Atheists to pious

Since the types seem to fall into approximately four percentiles, according to the books *Please Understand Me* and *Gifts Differing*, the brief profiles are given from the least to the greatest.

Introverted Intuitives
(1% of the Population)

INFJs-Empathizers
(Mostly Female)

Although INFJs—extremely protective and mother-hen like—make up only 1 percent of the nation, they wield much behind-the-scenes influence. They are very sensitive, serious, private, and quiet; able in many cases to pick up on illness and upset even before the victim does. They feel deeply and care genuinely. The attitude, "I'd rather make suggestions than decisions," characterizes most of them.

INFJs are willing to tolerate working with their hands or involvement with boring facts if it paves the way for them to help people emotionally, preferably one at a time. Like other intuitives, INFJs usually do not enjoy working with money, business, or physical details.

Sensing-thinking types offer INFJs the security and protection they need.

INFPs—Idealists
(Mostly Female)

INFPs are some of the most intellectually profound persons because their ideas are not in bondage to structure. Attracted to individual crisis and unstoppable in their commitment to personal involvement, INFPs sacrifice physically, financially, and emotionally—often beyond their own strength.

Although sensitive and analytical, INFPs shoot for the stars when they get hooked on a cause; yet they can sink to the depths of despair when that pursuit fails. No other type cares so deeply or fights so tenaciously as the INFPs. They quietly and effectively campaign for individual concerns, but when rebuke by word or pen is needed, INFPs rise to the occasion. Their writing can be soothingly lyrical or stingingly truthful.

INFPs are free-spirited and fiercely resist being put in a box or on a schedule. Cleaning house seems to repel INFPs more than any other chore, yet if the need arose, they would clean all day and do it well for someone else because their byline is, "When I'm doing something for someone else, it has to be done right."

Since INFPs are oblivious to overextension of themselves, structured-sensing, thinking types provide excellent seesaw balance.

INTJs—Expert Strategists
(Mostly Male)

INTJs can concentrate on possibilities and make situation-based, logical decisions with little regard for skeptics. They deplore wasting time, energy, money, ability, or supplies. INTJs compete with themselves, so they must always improve over the previous day's accomplishments. Therefore, many INTJs are perfectionists as well as workaholics.

Theory is their middle name, and brainstorming is their hobby. INTJs can sum up given facts and possibilities brilliantly and concisely on the spot.

Because their minds are always swirling with abstract ideas and deadlines, INTJs often present an unemotional, cold, uncaring, and all-business attitude, even toward family and friends. The INTJ female is likely to have a tough time finding a mate who is not intimidated by her reasoning intelligence.

If they can resist feeling inferior, extroverted sensing-feeling people provide a refreshing conscious world contact for INTJs.

INTPs—Think-Tank Experts
(Mostly Male)

The byline of INTPs is "ideas under construction." INTPs strive to be exact and original at the same time. Their sophisticated concentration ability and respect for intelligence sometimes projects an arrogant atmosphere, often intimidating people who conclude they are not as smart as the INTP.

INTPs prefer to think up solutions or design rather than carry out the routine details of physical creation. Consequently, the finishers often receive credit for the work of INTPs. Because they live and move in the impersonal analytical and logical world, INTPs are hard to understand and are often totally unaware of the needs and feelings of others.

Extroverted, sensing friends or emotional deciders offer a good balance for INTPs if the noise level is kept subdued and the crowd small.

Extroverted Intuitives
(5% of the Population)

ENFJs—Encouragers
(Mostly Female)

ENFJs like to help others—particularly adults—find solutions to their emotional and relationship problems, patiently donating many hours listening and offering tactful advice. They are natural counselors, teachers, speakers, and writers and are capable of drawing out any type. However, most ENFJs find that their least-favored activities are keeping financial records, handling boring physical detail, and wasting precious time on meaningless pursuits.

Since the hardest assignment of ENFJs seems to be gathering physical facts and then making logically based decisions and sticking with them, sensing-thinking types greatly complement them.

ENFPs—Catalysts
(Mostly Female)

ENFPs are full of enthusiastic ideas, but they are not driven to finishing projects. If the road to heaven were paved with good intentions, ENFPs would be certain to make it. However, the day has often passed before their ideas are carried out. The most generous of people with time and possessions, ENFPs often allow their friends to drain them mentally, physically, and financially.

ENFPs have a special problem finding something to hold to since they prefer the intangible and abstract and are also spontaneous. Although their boredom level is extremely low, they are fun to watch when they get a hot lead on solving an emergency relationship or emotional problem. They resemble kangaroos hopping from one involvement to the other, always with friends galore watching, following, and admiring.

Since ENFPs do not go to bed by the clock, they are likely to experience poor sleep and work habits because they enjoy talking all night, not wanting to miss a minute of intriguing banter. The promise of exciting dialogue easily lures them away from study, appointments, and certainly away from cleaning house.

Excitement and action are the bywords of ENFPs. "I massage rules," Louise teased. "There's always a way around any rule, and it's exciting to find that one tiny loophole."

ENFPs are likely to hold to physical facts and possessions loosely. They are lucky to find structured friends to keep them stable.

ENTJs—Head Chiefs
(Mostly Male)

ENTJs are best known for their structured vision. Without new challenges, they wither on the vine. They often carry out and receive credit for the ideas of spontaneous intuitives.

Because their vision of possibilities never ceases, ENTJs can become slave drivers of themselves and others. Always in charge, no matter where they are, ENTJs exude positive authority, reveling in directing subordinates, family—or spouse, even—to complete the job or program at hand. ENTJs *have* to lead. Success to them is bound up in responsible reputation and respect rather than possessions. Like other systematic thinkers, ENTJs find inefficiency and error in themselves and others intolerable.

For awareness of people's feelings and appreciation needs, ENTJs benefit from the constant reminder of their feeling-decision friends.

ENTPs—Powerful People-Movers
(Mostly Male)

Enthusiastically interested in everything—the more complex the better—ENTPs accept the "it can't be done" challenge head-on with excitement and competence, even without backup experience. Because they enjoy risks or the unexpected, they control emotional crisis problems with calmness and expertise, never doubting their ability to handle an impossible situation. Their attitude of "I know what's going on" offers much security to the more fearful crowd.

ENTPs need a people-related challenge that requires creative analysis. They prefer to design and set in motion a program that will solve the problems rather than be involved in repetitive individual conversations. As some of the most fascinating and witty conversationalists, ENTPs will often be the center of attention as they engage in and direct their much-loved discussions.

ENTPs are likely to transmit an air or arrogance because of their optimistic competence, but they can learn from sensing-feeling people the importance of investing time in developing personal interest and sensitivity toward those less confident, verbal, and secure.

Introverted Sensing
(6% of the Population)

ISFJs—Servers
(Mostly Female)

ISFJs are attracted to assisting and teaching one-on-one or small groups — especially children, the elderly, or needy. They are usually exact and patient with physical details, facts, and people, but prefer to have plenty of time to think things over, disliking radical or sudden changes. Although ISFJs are patient listeners, hearing relationship or emotional problems distresses and frustrates them unless they've learned workable solutions from past experiences. However, they come alive with service and suggestions when physical problems arise.

ISFJs are very loyal to institutions, bosses, and family—any recipients of their services—often going the extra mile. ISFJs are not only taken for granted, but people can easily take advantage of their goodness. But once they're fed up, they can't be budged.

Thinking intuitives, though very strong, offer a good balance for ISFJs.

ISFPs—Sympathizers
(Mostly Female)

ISFPs are like hummingbirds—now you see them, now you don't—resisting anyone who becomes too possessive of them. Sympathetic, extremely private, quiet, friendly, but free-spirited, ISFPs are the least understood of all types; yet people admire their spunky independence.

Experienced, colorful, alive, warm, free, and breezy describe ISFPs. But too much reasoning, boring routine, questioning, or dependence chases them away. Many would rather suffer mentally than share their feeling about themselves or their problems.

Most ISFPs can identify with people who are in a physical crisis. They are stronger because they *have* to be. Depression may plague them from time to time, but ISFPs spring back to reality through their play ethic and mottos, "Today is the most important day."

ISFPs benefit greatly from exposure to those who are extroverted, structured, and logical thinkers.

ISTJs—Conscientious Workers
(Mostly Male)

You are in good hands with ISTJs because they are decisive in practical matters, careful and dependable, working out of a strong sense of responsibility and duty. They stand behind what they say. More than anything, ISTJs want to be trusted. They are often perceived as pillars of strength.

ISTJs worry about not meeting the standards or filling the quota, striving for accuracy as well. Giving a good day's work for a good day's pay is normal behavior since they are loyal to institutions and are avid rule-keepers. Their expertise with detailed money facts can't be beat.

ISTJs reflect a sober, serious, and conservative character. Yet in their private lives they reveal much humor, love for play, and respect for family ties.

An extroverted, feeling-intuitive with an optimistic outlook and warmth toward people is an excellent balance for an ISTJ.

ISTPs—Unstoppable Operators
(Mostly Male)

Serious, quiet, but fiercely independent, ISTPs are difficult to get to know. "Don't tell me what to do!" is on their minds and often on their lips. They know how to tune people out.

When challenged by the physical process of their work, recreation, craftsmanship, or practice, ISTPs demonstrate unmatched zeal and skill.

Their favorite combination is individual risk or danger along with physical crisis requiring astute concentration and quick action, as in surfing, surgery, truck driving, performing, and rescuing.

They generally love the freedom of the outdoors, particularly where survival depends on strength and stamina. Inactivity is their worst enemy, causing them to become restless, depressed, irritable, and discouraged.

An ISTP female often has a difficult time adjusting to the humdrum, even-keel, penned-in life of a mother with small children. She will no doubt be compelled to find personal physical release through sports, music, or performance.

An extroverted, friendly, emotional decision-maker will complement the ISTP's standoffishness.

Extroverted-Sensing
(13% of the Population)

ESFJs—Hostesses and Hosts
(Mostly Female)

ESFJs are the most sociable of all types. They love people and conversation. They need both nearly all the time. "ESFJs would talk to a grizzly bear if it moved," one of their admirers conjectured.

ESFJs love to give intricate details down to who sneezed. They are excellent hosts and hostesses, making everyone physically and socially comfortable. They can talk with anyone who has shared like experiences, and most of them are willing to listen as well. "Quiet bothers me" accurately describes and ESFJ.

Because ESFJs know the facts and want to get things finished in the most efficient and harmonious manner and are comfortable with people, they can become somewhat bossy coaches and teachers who use the "war" words—*should, ought, must,* and *need.* Since they enjoy teaching routine facts, for most of them, little children are a must in their lives.

The careers of ESFJs must involve people and provide conversational opportunities. Otherwise they will become discouraged and empty.

Thinking intuitives are intrigued by ESFJs because they are so bubbly about facts and people.

ESFPs—Performers
(Mostly Female)

"Let's have a party," is often on the lips of ESFPs, who celebrate at the drop of an eyelash. They love social occasions, and the more people on hand the better.

ESFPs will most likely attract as well as entertain an audience. Gales of laughter will probably accompany their witty rehearsal of personal experiences or sharing of jokes. It's almost impossible to impose on an ESFP who is sitting on "go," ready for company, excitement, and fun—if you can find them at home, that is.

ESFPs enjoy life, but are careful to hide the parts they don't like. Because they want a trouble-free, optimistic life, they are easily influenced toward taking shortcuts to happiness. ESFPs have difficulty bearing up under trouble because they particularly relish lighthearted enjoyment of people, conversation, and occasions. "Life is to enjoy" is their motto. Their generous giving of time, money, and energy has no strings attached.

Although INTPs seem distant toward people and dislike frivolity, extroverted feeling types are a good balance for them.

ESTJs—Organizers
(Mostly Male)

ESTJs appreciate people. Wherever they are, ESTJs can't resist organizing those who will play games, carry out programs, or do the work. ESTJs are menders and builders, but not necessarily diplomatic about giving directions, nor do they lavish others with praise and appreciation. Their expertise lies in seeing the most systematic and expedient way of getting the job and activities accomplished. They expect no more of anyone else than they do of themselves. Hence, ESTJ bosses may show up in overalls and boots with toolbox in hand. They're not afraid of grime and dirt.

ESTJs can't rest until the job is finished. Therefore, if workers are absent, they will finish the job alone, usually without complaint or back patting. Consequently, many ESTJs join the workaholics' crowd. ESTJs also organize their possessions and schedules and want their family members to follow suit.

Like ISTJs, ESTJs are more loyal to institutions, work, and community than to people. They despise shirkers. Most of all, they want people to trust their judgment. ESTJ females are likely to carry tools in their purses.

Feeling-intuitives bring out the best in an ESTJ.

ESTPs—Rescuers
(Mostly Male)

ESTPs love people but can be very possessive of them, especially family. They want to be in charge and want their orders to be respected.

ESTPs are very conversational and are often on-stage as they share their wit, charm, and funny stories. ESTPs like to control the conversation, and they have the ability to aim it like an arrow or sharp dagger.

Since they thrive on physical crises, many of them direct rescue operations in their spare time or get involved in dangerous occupations. ESTPs know what to do in an emergency and can bark orders without hesitation. They know who is in charge—they are! They think and act quickly, demonstrating selflessness, courage, and nerves of steel. They never seem to tire of fighting the worst disaster.

ESTPs often use this emergency-handling ability to pull troubled companies or institutions out of the red very quickly and with finesse. But once the job is done, ESTPs prefer to move on to another emergency. Consequently, because they do not see their ideas to the final finish, ESTPs often are not credited with their ideas.

ESTPs are attracted to their opposites, feeling intuitives, who help modify their toughness.

Appreciating Differences

Identifying and remembering people's types shows respect, not only for their abstract right to develop along lines of their own choosing, but also for the concrete ways in which they are and prefer to be different from others.[3]

To understand personality types, we must respect who others are and accept their potential struggles. By examining differences in temperament, we can understand the reasons for unhappiness in the home, at school, and on the job.

Conflict and boredom are especially apparent in the modern workplace. Employees often are forced to work with persons either much like themselves or totally opposite their personality, with both situations presenting prime opportunity for interpersonal conflict. Similarly, inner conflict can result from performing tasks that are contrary to one's nature and temperament, thereby resulting in boredom and lack of initiative. Conflict both from external and internal sources can result in burnout.

Because this issue of burnout on the job is of particular interest in today's society, I have listed here some actual cases that have come to my attention.

•An INFP drilling holes for five and a half years
•An introvert working in a noisy, hustle-and-bustle office
•An extrovert working alone in a warehouse
•An intuitive attempting to do bookkeeping all day
•A thinking foreman whose workers consistently make costly mistakes
•A sensing person working where rules are constantly changing
•A structured person who doesn't know from one minute to the next what job he or she will be doing
•A spontaneous person who is penned inside with deadline projects
•An extroverted intuitive operating a radiology machine—small, boring, repetitive procedures
•An INFJ working in a noisy, rushed, hospital where time is inadequate to give complete care
•An ENTP tied to daily meetings
•A feeling judgment person responsible for firing employees
•A spontaneous person having to punch a time clock at 6 AM
•An ISTJ whose co-workers are constantly stirring up things
•An ESTP whose boss will not listen to economical suggestions
•An ENFJ who has access to no other intuitive
•An INTP locked to a repetitive operation procedure
•An ENTJ pastor whose congregation wants no changes
•An ESFJ who has a solitary job in a research library

Conclusion

Applying all this understanding of personality types at home, school, on the job, and in marriage can sweeten the oldest relationship and influence the newest. God delights in giving insight into behavioral patterns of others and for patience to allow others free expression. Jesus said, "I give you a new commandment, that you love one another. Just as I have loved you, you also should love one another" (John 13:34). Understanding promotes love.

The bicyclists are drawn together in one large group for introduction of group leaders, instructions, and review of safety rules, paralleling the grouping of various types in families, businesses, neighborhoods, churches, and schools. Only as they proceed on the trip do the riders realize their distinct differences or likenesses and how much they rely on each other.

Thank you, Father, for the temperament with which you gifted me. Help me learn to understand and and to appreciate my temperament and that of others.

Notes

[1]Gordon Lawrence, *People Types and Tiger Stripes* (Gainesville Fl: Center for Application of Psychological Type, 1979) 18.

[2]Isabel Briggs Myers and Peter B. Myers, *Gifts Differing* (Palo Alto CA: Consulting Psychologists Press, 1980) 206.

[3]Ibid., 10.

Chapter 12

Creative Compromise

Iron sharpens iron, and one person sharpens the wit of another.
—Proverbs 27:17

Although understanding and accepting God's design for ourselves and for others removes tension and improves our self-worth, putting this understanding to work in the most effective blending of temperaments demands creative compromise.

People are attracted to those who have strengths they do not have. Pinch points are either creative or competitive; we make the decision. Conflicts are camouflaged blessings that call for creative compromise that will ultimately, if dealt with wisely, strengthen a friendship.

According to Webster, compromise means "a settlement of differences in which each side makes concessions; blending qualities of two different things." As individual types are thrown together at random in school, families, friendship, employment, and church, conflicts and clashes are sure to occur.

If misunderstandings and dissensions were viewed merely as red flags that indicate legitimate and solvable differences calling for clarification and possibly compromise, . . . fewer young people would marry just to leave home . . . divorce lawyers would be looking for work . . . alcohol and drugs would lose their appeal . . . families would be closer . . . church fellowships would be friendlier and more effective. When you know yourself, you can tolerate the thoughtlessness or differences of others.

Blending Social Preferences

Compromising introversion and extroversion is really very simple. Extroverts need to listen more, respond less quickly, limit noise, and avoid drawing unnecessary attention to their introverted friends, children, students, and mates. They cannot assume that reserved introverts are bored, snobbish, sad, or mad. Being aware of the reluctance of many introverts to jump into a conversation, extroverts can invite their opinions.

Introverted mates usually feel very comfortable with extroverted mates who will carry the conversation. Yet, the extroverted mate really tires of doing all the taking and bearing the social load.

"I just hate it when John says to me in front of our friends, 'Bev, you haven't said two words all evening,' " Beverly complained. "I don't want our friends to think Bev is a numbskull," John defended. "She's got lots of good ideas, and I'm proud of her. But they don't know that." Beverly, like other introverts, could endeavor to talk a little more to put extroverts like her husband at ease, or at least smile intentionally to give positive signals.

Extroverts can help get introverts involved by being slower to respond, looking expectantly at their mate or friend for response, or priming the pump with "_____ has good ideas on this."

"I thought my wife wasn't talking in an argument because she knew she was wrong," Ralph said. "But now I see that her introversion doesn't speak as fast as my extroversion."

Extroverts should give introverts the option of writing down their objections rather than competing verbally with the extroverts' mountain of words. Extroverts often assume that introverts don't *want* to answer, when in fact, they are probably thinking over what or how to answer. Introverts can aid in compromise by saying, "I prefer to talk later."

"We're both introverted at our house," Ellen shared. "Before we go to work we say two things: 'good morning' and 'see ya.' We do our talking in the evenings—what little there is."

When extroverts know that co-workers are introverted, they won't "talk their ears off" or feel threatened by their morning reservation or assume they are grouchy. Introverts need time to warm up to the day.

Extroverts will be less critical of a pessimistic outlook when they consider that someone is speaking (or not speaking) from natural introversion. Introverts become more extroverted when they accept their introversion. Conversely, it should help the easily outgoing to modify their inclination to comment on everything.

"Now that I know I'm an introvert," Wade said, "I find I am less annoyed by my dim view of things. Some of my friends can see the change. I just don't worry like I used to."

Extroverts can demonstrate appreciation of introverts' need for privacy by allowing them to pull away from the crowd and have silent times during the day and plenty of time to be alone.

Parents can teach children while they are very young to be sensitive to the social preferences of others. Loquacious children can be taught the appropriate time for talk if one or both of their parents is introverted.

Schoolteachers are obligated to draw introverted children out. Many students of this type must be forced to recite, but teachers can be sensitive to their fears and allow them as much spontaneous reaction as possible.

Church school teachers can promise their students that only volunteers will read or pray aloud. People don't *have* to go to Sunday school or church. We have learned why many people prefer to be in a large, lecture-type class: they fear that they will be asked a question they can't answer. Some of these are extroverts, but most are introverts who prefer to listen rather than respond.

Introverts need not assume that just because extroverts talk a lot and seem very confident that they always feel that way. So, reaching out to extroverts—taking a calculated risk—is a mature compromise for introverts.

Cautious introverts need to welcome confident extroverts, knowing that they, too, are sensitive about whether or not they are accepted. Everyone lacks confidence in some areas, but extroverts cover their lack with words, while introverts often openly lack confidence.

Introverts can learn to be patient with their extroverted friends, co-workers, and spouses who trip over their tongues. Some introverts discount everything extroverts say, which isn't fair. Given the option to trade processes, introverts probably would not. Many extroverts claim they wish they were introverts. Introverts sometimes declare they would give anything to be extroverted, but when all is said and done, not many would really trade. We can all learn from the opposite preferences, though.

Although blending introversion and extroversion calls for constant compromise as each person considers the needs of the other, failure to blend would produce a very colorless world.

Blending the Information-Gathering Process

The difference between sensing and intuition is critical, causing most of the difficulty and disagreement between friends, in marriages and families, with co-workers, and at church. But communication based on understanding and appreciation paves the way for creative compromise, or companionship.

When an idea-person and a physical-world-person put their heads together, they come up with a clear picture. The intuitive will recommend many possibilities, and the sensing person will gather facts. However, in an argument, they get no place because they don't speak the same language. A good compromise in this partnership is not to expect the intuitive to do an inordinate amount of repetitious physical work or endure a completely factual dialogue.

"I finally realized what really bugs me about Phil," Tina sighed. "His love for facts drives me crazy after a while. I listen to his phone conversations with his business associates and just have to leave the room because I can't stand to hear prices, times, weights, and details. I realize that my scattered skimming of facts must frustrate him just as much."

To compromise, Phil could limit his fact-giving when Tina is obliged to listen, and Tina could gain more respect for facts.

To avoid infringing on the personal time of sensing friends or family members, intuitives can limit long counseling phone conversations and resist lengthy detainment after meetings and classes. Intuitives can also refrain from asking sensing persons to endure long, abstract discussions on behavior.

A compromise can be reached by writing down ideas, giving sensing persons ample time to read and consider. Sensing persons can ease tension by not pressing intuitives for details they do not care about retaining. Intuitives can endeavor to give the chronological facts that sensing people prefer. Compromise is possible, but expecting these two mind types to work in an identical way is a dream.

Compromise is attained when sensing persons are no longer intimidated by the intuitives' natural air of authority that comes from their retention of ideas and problem-solving ability. When an intuitive appreciates and respects a sensing person's product-and-service contributions and common-sense suggestions, each can rely on the other when the situation warrants.

None of us should put another down for what that type is not comfortable doing. We should allow everyone to use their peculiar gifts in the proper spot. For example, sensing people need latitude in handling financial concerns and details and logistics of a situation. Because intuitives are best at problem-solving, staying abreast of relationship problems, and looking ahead to what might happen, they need to be in charge in such situations.

Employers can compromise by putting intuitive workers in places of variety and challenge, and by placing sensing workers where duties will be fairly steady and detailed.

Taking into consideration the fact-gathering preferences of children, parents and teachers can do much to raise their self-esteem by assuring them that no one is able in every area.

Once sensing persons know that intuitives become restless from time to time when the challenge is gone, they can be willing to make changes more often. Intuitives, understanding that sensing people like repetition and dislike change, can temper their hunger for variety.

Boredom ruins many friendships, though it is sometimes difficult to distinguish between boredom and oppositeness. When two people prefer the same fact-gathering process, competition and boredom are likely to disrupt friendship. Therefore, two sensing people need to consider and accept each other's common-sense facts, whereas two intuitives need to give each other the opportunity to express ideas.

When a sensing person realizes what potential an intuitive possesses and an intuitive realizes the common sense the opposite type possesses, the blend is harmonious—a plus for any business, family, marriage, or church.

Blending the Decision-Making Process

Although blending impersonal situation-based decisions with emotional people-based decisions often stirs up a lot of conflict and hurt feelings, creative compromise can solicit the best from each perspective and present strong and warm balanced decisions. The impersonal thinking process brings logic to personal relationships; the emotional process brings feelings—both necessary for success and meaningful existence.

Often, compromise decisions require much dialogue and open sharing of feelings, desires, and hurts, grounded in the basic self-esteem and confidence of both parties.

People who rely on logic usually do not care to discuss matters for long; they assume their decisions are the most practical. These strong deciders can compromise by admitting that even when they think they are right, they may not be totally correct. They can, at least, give feeling people a chance to express their ideas. If logical thinkers would entertain free exchange of ideas more often, in many cases the flow of tears and hurt feelings would subside. People often cry when they feel defeated, inferior, or unimportant.

"After I've cleaned all day," Martha said, "Dan comes in and inspects it all, usually finding several things wrong. When I asked him why he never points out the good things and shows appreciation for them, he said, 'When I don't say anything, that's a sign you are doing it right. I'll just tell you when you are doing it wrong. So, you can go ahead and appreciate what you've done when I don't mention anything!' I reject that," Martha said.

There is nothing particularly spiritual about allowing people to walk all over you, withholding the appreciation you need, but feeling people should be careful not to put a peace price tag on every decision or attempt to put guilt trips on people who fail to meet their expectations. However, logical thinkers, who are informed about the sensitivity of feeling people and their need for approval, can compromise by not taking advantage of their soft-heartedness or burdening them with undue criticism, and by being a little more understanding and generous with appreciation and encouragement.

People who think logically can encourage compromise by not projecting the attitude that feeling people are inferior or weak. There's no particular merit in a one-vote home, office, or friendship—except for the absence of disagreement. Those who judge intellectually can encourage compromise by not pushing ideas off on those who judge emotionally and tend to give in easily in deference to peace and harmony.

Feeling people who acknowledge their mixed emotions regarding people-based decisions can benefit from the suggestions of logical thinkers, and compromise will bring about the wisest decision. This method works both ways, for logical thinkers are wise to consider the heartfelt considerations of feeling people. Emotional people can calm troubled waters by modifying their accusations of coldness and selfishness toward logical people.

"When my thinking wife is about to come home from work," said Joe, an emotional decider, "I get uptight wondering about what I haven't done or what she's going to bark about when she comes in all tired and grouchy. The kids and I hate to see her coming." This grouchy wife had no idea that her husband was so intimidated. She thought he just wasn't willing to talk and be nice to her. But after she heard his fears, she said, "I can change that easily! I didn't know he was afraid of me."

Feeling persons can compromise by considering the logical decisions and suggestions of others, even though they go against the grain. Emotional decisions are not always right, nor are logical decisions. Putting the two processes together before making a final decision promises wisdom and warmth in most situations.

Logical persons, especially introverts, will not have the same need for people as emotional persons. A compromise here would be to include people more often, knowing that the feeling friend or spouse needs approval.

Comparing Lists

Logical deciders seem to have two lists, one for situations and one for people, while emotional deciders keep one list of people intermingled with situations, such as job. Usually the feeling person's spouse heads the single list, and the logical person's spouse undoubtedly heads the people list. However, because the logical decider tends to separate situation and people and because he has such a strong sense of responsibility to his job, it can appear that career and responsibility to children are placed ahead of spouse. The logical thinker assumes that the spouse understands and agrees with the necessity of duty to job and children. In reality, however, that spouse is likely to feel neglected and unimportant—on the bottom of the list.

In the happy situation where the logical partner considers the feeling spouse a source of pleasure rather than of duty, she may in fact (in keeping with the sense of responsibility) not "allow" herself enough of the pleasure component (the spouse). This is almost certain to be taken negatively and compound the problem; it is unlikely to be interpreted as the backhanded compliment it may really be. Therefore, it behooves the logical person to increase his awareness of the desirability of purposely placing spouse above situations at times and taking care that family members who are important to him do not feel taken for granted.

Feeling decision-makers do not mind making logic-based decisions if everyone is pleased. Therefore, a compromise would be for logically oriented persons to support emotion-based decisions whenever possible.

When a thinking person patiently supports a feeling person's people-based decisions and helps her work through mixed emotions, he is doing three things—lifting the person's self-worth, increasing her self-confidence, and putting her in touch with her own logical process. In the same way, when an emotional person acknowledges the wisdom of logical judgments and shows appreciation for their stability, the logically inclined will become less defensive of his authority.

When both sides are comfortable about who they are, compromising on decision making will happen automatically and effectively.

Blending Lifestyle Preferences

Although most difficulties in relationships stem from the difference in styles of gathering information, many of the irritating nuisances that grow in hostility, bitterness, and resentment stem from God-designed lifestyle differences. Creative compromise is easiest in this area since the world is divided about 50/50 between the spontaneous and the structured lifestyle, giving each side plenty of company. Compromise means allowing another to partially influence you, knowing that what the other person prefers is something you probably need to learn anyway.

Because of lifestyle preference, there can be great tension between parent and child or teacher and child. Teaching a structured child to form good habits is much easier than teaching an unstructured child. Attempting to organize or keep a spontaneous child on a regular schedule frustrates both parties. The key is to influence and encourage children when schedule or organization is absolutely essential without trying to change their basic nature. Unstructured children will also benefit from understanding why they are not more organized, and can thus avoid feeling inferior and second-class.

A very difficult situation often arises when a structured parent lives with an unstructured spouse and children. When the spontaneous mate realizes the stresses on the structured mate, he or she can encourage the children to cooperate and get things done. Remembering that spontaneous people respond best to emergency situations will keep the structured parent from assuming that this type of spontaneous support will be constant. If the organized mate doesn't expect the spontaneous members of the family to get things finished on a structured time schedule, then disappointment and resentment can be avoided and cooperation achieved.

Compromise might also include avoiding giving orders to the spontaneous mate. Parent-like statements have no place in a marriage. Substituting "I prefer" or "I would appreciate" for *you should, ought, must,* and *need* keeps marriage on an adult basis. A structured person is wise to allow the unstructured person to introduce play and relaxation into their life together.

A significant and painful clash often occurs when a structured, logical husband assumes and demands that his unstructured wife keep a tidy house or maintain a by-the-clock meal schedule. Many divorces stem from this one major difference. Many women have sought outside employment to escape their dislike of boring housework. This type husband will want to avoid authority statements and assist his wife with the mundane duties she detests. Such a compromise will not sacrifice his inborn appetite for authority.

In finances, the spontaneous spouse may want to take risks over the objection of the structured mate who wants everything paid off in full and nothing to be wasted. Compromise can involve a little risk to satisfy one and a good amount of security to satisfy the other. One husband's financial risk upset his structured wife to the point of causing serious marriage problems, so in order to compromise, the husband agreed to consult a financial planner.

In planning activities, an unstructured person could compromise by not dropping last-minute plans on his structured family, while a structured person could learn to be more flexible over unavoidable last-minute changes. A good blend between these two types gives a relationship great resources for emergency, as well as routine, happenings. Patience and trust with each other is the key.

Concerning schedules, it is a courteous gesture to allow a spontaneous person to be unstructured when there is no real need to be time conscious. Likewise, it is considerate to give a structured person freedom to rely on the clock and complete a list of jobs. Such tolerance will guarantee individual expression and produce harmony. Spouses who differ in these areas are set to handle crises as well as routines.

For example, when a spontaneous person and a structured person decide to undertake a project together, perhaps paint a room, the structured person usually intends to start first thing in the morning. The spontaneous person wants to start right away, even if it's 10 PM, preferring to paint all night. A compromise would be for the structured person to give in to the spontaneous person's preference, if tomorrow he would not be totally devastated by the lack of sleep. Or, the spontaneous person might agree to start painting in the morning—not at 7 AM, but when she got up—and to continue painting throughout the day, but stopping for meals.

In the workplace, spontaneous and structured people might clash over which shifts they prefer, since structured people usually enjoy working first and being off later. Compromises can be made to satisfy each a little. Structured people can avoid obligating the unstructured to meetings on top of meetings. Yet, the unstructured, knowing that meetings are necessary evils, can discipline themselves to attend some meetings without total surrender of their preference. A spontaneous person hates to be hemmed in, while an organized person feels more secure tied to a schedule. To compromise, each could give a little on occasion or take turns.

A structured person, though often envied by the unstructured person, can learn from the unstructured how to play and relax. Finishing projects is not the greatest virtue in the world, nor is playing first and working later the worst fault. Thinking that another's preference is inferior is probably the worst temptation for us all. Keep in mind that being locked to the clock is just as hard for a spontaneous person as being completely flexible and unorganized is for a structured person. Adjusting to one another's lifestyle differences, though requiring good communication based on respect and trust, really contributes variety, fun, and maturity, and is well worth the struggle.

Conclusion

As we cycle together, it's no secret that several bikers are having spats. The spontaneous riders are off on private little jaunts or popping wheelies, upsetting the feeling riders who fear accidents. Quite a few sensing cyclists are way behind because they've stopped to wade in a stream and pick up pretty rocks. Because they have been so engrossed in conversation, several feeling parents have lost track of their children. An intuitive rider is coasting along slowly beside another biker while they discuss a personal problem. A group of sensing bikers has sped way ahead to gather wood for a huge bonfire. Several intuitive members have parked their bikes in a grassy area where they are planning the evening's program following the wiener roast. Everyone seems to be having a super time.

We marvel, Father, at your wisdom in creating so many different types of people. Give us understanding so we may appreciate each one.

Chapter 13

Finding the Weight of Your Confidence

For the Lord will be your confidence and will keep your foot from being caught.
　　　　　　　　　　　　　　　　　　—Proverbs 3:26

When people discover who they are as individuals and understand why they do certain things in a particular way and how they fit into society, and that it is all by God's design, their self-esteem is bound to zoom upward. It also becomes easier for them to appreciate why others approach ideas and actions in opposite ways. Such understanding eases tension and promotes creative compromise, all positive steps toward unity. However, there are still inner forces fighting to prevent personal self-worth and confidence. Among these are the following:

- •Unsuitable jobs
- •Unhappy marriages
- •Lack of education
- •Spiritual poverty

- •Family reputation
- •Alcohol and drug abuse
- •Immature mistakes
- •Obesity

While all these are serious problems that can be solved in time by changing one's way of thinking, obesity is the only one that is visible to the naked eye. One of the most common problems in America, obesity contributes to feelings of inferiority, depression, and lack of self-confidence.

It would be wonderful to be understood and appreciated for who we are. However, most of us yearn to be something else—5'5", 105 pounds, and beautiful, or 6'2", 180 pounds, and muscular—to insure immediate respect and admiration.

"Do you have any idea what it's like to choose a restaurant by the size of the booth rather than by menu or atmosphere?" Julia questioned. When someone's weight restricts where they can go, how far they can walk, what they can play, how long or where they can work, or the style of clothes they can wear, they have every reason to be angry with their self-imposed handicap.

One of the first things someone with renewed self-esteem will want to do is get their body into shape so that it does not hinder use of their gifts. If people would learn to use their gifts to the fullest, there would be no need to impress others with power, prestige, or accomplishments or to apologize for inabilities. However, the way we look sometimes becomes a barrier between the respect of others and our self-confidence.

Since getting rid of excess weight and toning our bodies is a big part of liking how we look and improving our opinion of ourselves, we will discuss how applying our God-designed preferences can assist in finding the weight of our confidence.

Appearance and Respect

"I'm not what I look like," Felicia said. "I really like myself, now that I see how and why God designed me the way He did. But all this weight has to go. How can I hope to help others with their problems if my appearance says to them that I have little discipline in my own life? I may be able to convince them after a while that I know what I'm talking about, but the barriers to cross to get to that point waste time and effort."

Sometimes the way people look is a consequence of their previous low opinion of themselves. "I was miserable," Felicia continued, "so I buried my sorrows in food. Then I'd see how awful I looked and hate myself so much, I'd eat to comfort myself. Food was my pacifier. It could have been gambling, booze, or sleeping around, I suppose. I want people to respect me now that I respect myself. I've got to fix up this 'ole bod,' " she grinned.

The way we look certainly affects the respect we get from others, especially people who do not know us, though sometimes even the people who do know and love us withhold respect.

"I was amazed at how differently my relatives treated me after I lost 30 pounds," Sonja said. " 'Why, you're normal,' an aunt said. It really angered me to see their level of respect increase. I had become someone important just because I was thin. I vowed then and there that I would never allow extra pounds to rob me of respect for others."

Obese people lack respect for other obese people. Case in point: A very large female friend and I were attending a meeting when another heavy woman came down the aisle. "Isn't she fat?" my friend sneered. I hardly knew what to say. Usually you see those faults in others that you have yourself, but I didn't say that.

Some things about our appearance we cannot help—for example, our facial features, bone structure, and height—but people who have healthy self-esteem usually have little problem accepting and adjusting to what was assigned to them. Nearly everyone would like to make some changes if they could. However, removing excess weight is something within our control.

Weight and Self-Esteem

"I feel inferior when I'm around thin girls," Debbie groaned. "They have more going for them. People like them better, and they really have more reason to be happy." Lie-number-one is: "I don't measure up to the trim, attractive, assertive girls." Other lies follow:

• "Heavy-set people are not as much fun."
• "I have nothing to offer."
• "I'm missing out on life."
• "I'll never attract the opposite sex."
• "I'll probably never get married."

When people allow weight to warp their self-esteem, a poor self-image will nullify much of their potential.

Alice, a woman whose self-esteem has risen 100 percent since she discovered her God-given temperament and who now likes herself, has shed much excess weight. "I used to look at myself as odd," she reflected, "but now I look at myself as unusual. All the gifts God gave me, I had learned *not* to use."

When you discover you're okay as a person, then you can get rid of the false face of weight, or at least modify it.

"Even though I still want to lose 50 pounds," Alice mused, "in my mind I'm thin already. My body will just have to catch up with my mind." Alice now has an abundance of friends, her life is full of happy activities, and she's reaching out to others who are struggling with the overweight problem due to low self-esteem.

Find the weight where you feel your best physically and emotionally. You may be thicker in the waist than your sister or even your mother, but health is more important than looks. If you like who you are and 20 or so extra pounds don't inhibit your "stage presence" or your activities, you've found the weight of your confidence. But if that excess baggage is a deterrent to your confidence, analyzing the reasons behind your weight may help you whip the problem.

Some people eat because they are bored or because they are tense about transition from one activity to another. Others crave food when they are nervous or anxious. Analyzing the time factor has helped many become aware of these snack traps.

Because introverts tend to withdraw and internalize their fears of failure and feelings of inferiority, they make friends of their food. Their intake of extra calories is often behind closed doors.

"Before I liked who I was," Beth explained, "I allowed myself to become fat because it was easier to suppose that people disliked me because I was fat than because of my personality. I always knew I could get rid of the fat, but I was stuck with my inferior personality. What if I got thin and nobody liked me anyway? was a question that plagued me and kept me eating."

Extra weight is a type of security in some cases. "I'm purposely overweight," one portly male teacher explained, "because those kids wouldn't respect me if I were skinny. I've got to put a certain amount of scare into them, or I couldn't control the classroom."

Yet, how does one explain that a tiny confident woman can control a rowdy bunch of bored high schoolers? Authority and confidence are not tied to weight, although a big person may initially discourage misbehavior or intimidate young children.

There is another side to the spectrum. "I don't have enough confidence to be overweight," Leslie admitted. "I guess I'm that vain, but if I think I bulge, I can't keep my mind on what I'm trying to teach."

Studies on attitudes toward weight indicate that the amount of fat on someone's body is an index of the amount of control they feel they have secured over other aspects of their lives.

Attitude Toward Food

Often we have to change our thinking toward our food background before we can get a stranglehold on excessive food intake.

"I was brought up on a farm," Ronnie said. "We got up early, ate a huge breakfast, and worked hard all day. Every meal was a large meal, but we worked it off." There's a difference in the food requirements of someone who handles a jackhammer and someone who pushes a pencil.

"Every happy memory—what few there were—of my childhood involved food," Wanda reminisced. "When I eat, I get that same old feeling of special treatment.

"When we were little, food was a reward for being good. Mother bribed us with food in exchange for good behavior. Her purse always held special treats in church. Now when I want to pat myself on the back for an accomplishment, I eat.

"Eating became a consolation to me when anyone mistreated me. After pouring myself out for family and friends or allowing people to walk all over me without a shred of appreciation or thanks, I'd console myself with a banana split. 'See, I love you,' I'd tell myself."

Psychologist Albert Ellis says, "You don't need what you want." When we want an ice cream sundae, no matter how hot the weather is, we really don't need it.

Extroverts may use food as a substitute for people or as a come-on to get a crowd together. "Let's go get a pizza," usually falls on willing ears. Extroverts don't necessarily want the pizza, but the conversation. Extroverts who like to throw and attend parties usually are tempted to overindulge in the glitter and glue that attract people to parties—snacks and food.

"I've made this four-layer German chocolate cake and need someone to help us eat it," puts a luscious guilt trip on relatives and friends. If we eat a piece, we can't blame ourselves for making the hostess feel good. After all, hearing people rave about their culinary creations is a large contributor to their self-esteem.

Problems with Losing Weight

"Why can't I lose weight?" Cynthia asked. "I like myself; I enjoy what I do; I like being around people. I'm disciplined in every area of my life except my weight. I love to talk and have made myself refrain from talking for hours at a time, but I can't make myself control the intake of food." Cynthia, like many middle-aged people, has missed the subtlest reason for weight gain. She has decreased activities without decreasing food intake.

Are you eating the same amount as you did when you worked on the combine in the sweltering July heat? Are you eating the same quantity as you did when you were jumping out of bed after only six hours of sleep, fixing breakfast, furiously packing lunches, running up and down the stairs, and hurrying the children off to school, then meeting them after school (missing your nap of course), going to school activities, playing ball with them, and on and on and on?

As we grow older, we don't realize the gradual slowdown in physical responsibilities and continue to eat the same amount. There are fewer clothes to wash and fold and put away, less cooking to do, fewer dishes to wash and put away, less pick-up of clutter, not as much bending, less cleaning, vacuuming, dusting, bed-making, and more sleep because we don't have to roll out as early or wait up as late. There is more eating out, fewer groceries to buy, and less hassle in cooking.

Because forming habits is so difficult for spontaneous people, demanding organized action in keeping track of calorie intake meal-by-meal, it leaves them cold and discouraged. Many spontaneous people reject imposed regulations about rigid diets anyway.

"I couldn't stand it when someone at the diet program would scold me for eating something I knew I shouldn't have," Andrea griped.. "I reported it, didn't I? I could have left it off! I didn't tabulate what I ate just for someone to ridicule my breaking the rules. I knew where I had fallen short. I didn't need someone to tell me. So, I would go on an eating binge when I got home because I felt like I had been verbally mistreated."

"I have to find something that rewards me more than food does," Tana said. "The byproducts of losing weight—a healthier heart, increased physical activity, decreased risk of diabetes, better looks—aren't important to a fat person. Everyone looks at me as being fat, so I might as well be. Fat people do not consider all the byproducts of being thinner as motivating enough to quit eating." The motivation for Tana to lose weight was to feel better and have more confidence.

"If I could consider ice cream cones and candy bars a perversion of food, or absolute no-no's like beer, cigarettes, and liquor, I think I could whip my problem," Martha reasoned.

Unstructured people may prefer to set aside a day's approved food supply and then munch whenever they get hungry. Studies show that people who spread their food out in little meals all through the day tend to be thinner than those who consume the same quantity of food on a regular three-meals-a-day basis.

Structured people, who are more organized and enjoy keeping records, may be able to restrain their food intake by keeping a count of calories meal-by-meal. Generally, they don't mind the restrictive rules of a weight-control club.

"What do I want most?" Martha pondered. "To lose weight or to eat. How can I have both of what I want most?" Anyone can have them both by mixing a little common sense with a dash of discipline. But before you design your own weight-loss program, it is wise to have a physical checkup to see if some medical problem is causing your weight gain.

How to Shape Up

When people have the proper reason to lose weight—for their own self-confidence and to feel good—the method for shaping up will be tailored according to their God-given temperament.

Sensitive people often want to trim down to gain the approval of someone. However, if someone adjusts their weight to please another, should that person ever reject or disappoint the dieter, the unwanted weight will probably come back very quickly. The first rule for losing weight is to want to take it off for your own pleasure. Naturally you will please others who are concerned about your appearance and self-confidence. Many Christians are helped by making weight loss a spiritual venture, profiting from classes such as "First Place" or "Free to Be Thin."

"Ephesians 5:28 says to love your wife as your own body," Henry sermonized. "I hated my fat body, and I realized that my attitude toward my wife was just about that poor. So I determined to lose 58 pounds for my own self-worth as well as for my wife."

God loves us whether we weigh 120 or 420 pounds. Our problem is loving ourselves.

When we love and respect ourselves, it's natural to want to improve our physical health. Diets repel most people, and we know from testimonies of those who have tried various crash diets that permanent results aren't realized. The best approach, then, changes from straining to reach a certain size or weight to striving to maintain a healthy body. It's no secret that the way we feel physically affects our mental, spiritual, and social attitude. The simple things we do faithfully on a daily basis with exercise and food consumption is the key to good health, which is so necessary for healthy self-esteem. Following is a simple plan for achieving maximum health.

Look at your schedule. Take a look at your schedule and the level of your physical energy output. If you are middle-aged and still eating as you did when your children were young or when you kept up with teenagers or did lots of physical labor, perhaps all you need to do is cut down on serving sizes. Keeping the word "decrease" on your lips as you eat will help you to revamp your eating habits. Eat only until you are full.

Observe your eating habits. When do you eat? Only at regular mealtimes? While you watch TV? Between meals? For a few days, record exactly what you eat and when. You may discover you're eating the right things, but at the wrong time. The idea that "breakfast is silver, lunch is gold, and dinner is lead" has helped me. Limiting desserts to before 4:00 in the afternoon allows your body to burn up the calories before bedtime.

The only safe and effective way to lose weight and keep it off is to reduce caloric intake by 500-1,000 calories per day and to make sure that you eat enough protein, low carbohydrates, fats, vitamins, and minerals. Crash dieting may appeal to those people who want immediate results, but there are no shortcuts to attaining and maintaining weight control. Eat slowly, make every meal an occasion, take smaller portions, and choose foods that take more time to eat—such as soup, fresh vegetables, and fruit. Also, drink 6 to 8 glasses of water a day, a necessity for proper functioning of your system.

Examine your pantry. Exactly what are you eating? Does your grocery shopping list reveal that every day you are getting the five basic groups of food—meat, milk, grains, vegetables, and fruits? Eating 5-7 servings of fruits and vegetables daily is a good plan. "You are what you eat" is not an empty slogan.

If you do not have a workable knowledge of nutrition, do some reading on how to prepare balanced meals quickly and economically. Read cookbooks, visit the library, or purchase a guide to nutrition. Monthly magazines often carry excellent articles on nutrition and meal planning.

A diet workshop friend advised simply, "If you will avoid three things— flour, sugar, and oil—you'll improve nutrition and trim away calories." Read the ingredients printed on food packaging. Eliminate as much sugar in your diet as you can. I've heard it said: "Watch the white stuff—refined sugar and flour."

Disciplined grocery buying may be all you need. Avoid shopping for groceries when you're hungry—i.e., when all the sweet things, tantalizing pastries, and luscious snacks (oil, flour, and sugar) are likely to play havoc with your good judgment.

Repeating the old adage, "A minute on your lips, forever on your hips," does wonders to restore perspective as displays catch your eye and irresistible aromas tease your appetite. Many of the quick-fix or heat-and-eat meals are loaded with hidden calories (sugar), in addition to being extremely expensive.

Shop by a list and stick to it—a little harder for unstructured people, but an excellent discipline. It's hard to write down "*one* bag of cookies, candy, or snacks" without a slight twinge of conscience.

"My family expects all those snacks and sweet things," Stella argued. "We pack lunches, you know." Children rely on parents to teach them about pet care, hygiene, and care of possessions, and they will eventually accept your judgment on food also. Our children were between the ages of 8 and 16 when we took a solid look at our food intake. I prided myself on serving well-balanced meals, but after we as a family read some nutrition books, the children respected what we learned about the side-effects of too much sugar, flour, and high calories—low nutrition dishes. Our attitude of improvement rather than restriction was contagious. Substituting raisins or fruit for cupcakes and chips was a matter of changing their thinking and of disciplined grocery buying.

Exercise and Tone. Increasing exercise without increasing food intake is the wisest way to reach the weight of your confidence. Bodies are designed to stretch, jump, bend, twist, grip, kick, stoop, and walk. Daily toning and stretching exercises not only will redistribute what you have, but also will be good therapy for mental stress. Walk each day—rain or shine, snow or sleet, hot or cold. You'll be amazed at how few colds you will contract.

Walking is one of the most pleasant ways to tone your muscles. It reduces the size of your stomach, improves your breathing, gives you fresh air and sunshine, and is good therapy for depression. Walking also offers excellent conditions for visiting with God or a companion and for enjoying the beautiful world God created. (Of course, some walkers prefer to soak up the moon and stars.) It's not how far you walk that matters, but how long you walk. Thirty minutes a day is the minimum. But walking is so delightful and makes your body feel so cared for that if you neglect going, your body will silently cry out. Some people prefer to run or jog—to each his own. Many fine books are on the market to guide you in your choice, but walking is absolutely safe. People who decide emotionally may want to find a walking buddy, since they usually don't like to do things alone. Walking may be too tame or organized for unstructured people, who may prefer to swim or ride bikes. (Did you know that cycling outdoors uses about half as many calories per mile as walking?)

Yoga and aerobics classes (and videotapes) have become very popular in recent years. They are a good addition to our sedentary lives. These classes are are offered at many different hours of the day and evening. Aerobics are not just for the young and agile. I know many grandmothers taking aerobics who declare they have never felt better in their lives. One lady said she now refuses any help up and down the stairs because she gets around so much better. Making new friends is another bonus from a class like this.

Celebrate. Keep track of your weight and measurements—not to compare yourself with a movie star, but to know when to celebrate. Reward yourself when you've lost inches or pounds: Go shopping—not for food, but for a new outfit. Treat yourself to an extra round of golf. Go to a movie. Above all, tell yourself that you "did good." Post your "grade" or top honors on the refrigerator.

Conclusion

Don't be surprised as you gain self-esteem and arrive at your weight of confidence if friends, family, and co-workers treat you differently. Often when people make significant progress or change, it upsets the balance of power. Others no longer feel superior, and they don't know what to do about it. Many people feel threatened when others move on to a more fulfilled life.

As you combine increased self-esteem with finding the weight of your confidence, you are equipped to get to the most important privilege of your life—influencing others toward a more fulfilling life.

In our crowd of bikers we admire those who have courageously determined to embark on a daily plan for increasing their exercise and improving their general health.

Thank you, Father, for the marvelous bodies and minds you have given us and for the privilege of using our energies in ways that benefit your kingdom.

Chapter 14

Humility—
The Missing Link

The fear of the Lord is life indeed.
—Proverbs 19:23

Understanding and appreciating personality types can raise self-esteem to a healthy level, foster better communication with others, strengthen studies, and facilitate career choice and mate selection. Yet, lasting happiness and deep personal fulfillment rest on having humility—the missing link in meaningful living and loving.

A medical doctor shares, "For hours I listen to people's ailments and ills. All are nontreatable illnesses because they are sick at heart. They don't know who they are or why they're here or how to be in a happy existence in this world."

Above all else, people are seeking peace of mind—which cannot be purchased, earned, awarded, built, borrowed, saved, or swallowed. Unfortunately, many do not discover the futility of human pursuits until their lives are half spent.

Several years ago the sociology department of Duke University did a study on requisites for peace of mind, the results of which have had wide circulation. Among the findings are:

• Avoid suspicion and resentment. Nursing a grudge is a major factor in unhappiness.
• Don't live in the past. An unwholesome preoccupation with old mistakes and failures leads to depression.
• Don't waste time and energy fighting conditions you cannot change. Cooperate with life instead of trying to run away from it.
• Force yourself to stay involved with the living world. Resist the temptation to withdraw and become reclusive during periods of emotional stress.

•Refuse to indulge in self-pity when life hands you a raw deal. Accept the fact that nobody gets through life without some sorrow and misfortune.
•Cultivate old-fashioned virtues—love, honor, compassion, and loyalty.
•Don't expect too much of yourself. When there is too wide a gap between self-expectation and your ability to meet the goals you have set, feelings of inadequacy are inevitable.
•Find something bigger than yourself to believe in. Self-centered, egotistical people score lowest in any test for measuring happiness.

These are excellent guidelines, but impossible for anyone to follow without holy help. Even if we could by our own strength avoid resentment, forget the past, cooperate with life, avoid depression, and have a positive attitude, still, without the proper spiritual view toward ourselves and others, our lives would be meaningless. Finding something bigger than ourselves to believe in is more expansive than a challenging career or community cause.

Expectations—
The Path to Resentment and Defeat

Even those people who have high self-esteem suffer disappointment when expectations are unmet, careers lack challenge, financial stability doesn't satisfy, mates withhold understanding and encouragement, and children fail to appreciate and honor parents.

A closer look at the expectations we put on ourselves and on others should ease some tensions. Expectation is a subtle form of manipulation. We expect people to attend weddings, funerals, and reciprocate dinner invitations. We have unspoken expectations and want others to guess what we want them to say and do.

The Scripture says, "Do to others as you would have them do to you" (Matt 7:12). It says nothing about assurance that those particular others would be obligated or inclined to return your favors.

"I was really upset when I visited my niece and she had no meal ready," Evelyn complained. "I had entertained her family royally just weeks before." Evelyn was unconsciously expecting her niece to return her favors. When the niece didn't comply, resentment crept in. Good relationships are far more important than returned hospitality.

Expecting married children to spend holidays at home is often the source of family tension. "I fixed Easter dinner for the whole crew," Janice moaned, "and not one of those kids brought me a flower, a box of candy, or anything. It's just not worth the trouble." Her children didn't know she expected a gift. Had Janice prepared that meal simply because she wanted to, there would have been no hidden expectations to lead to resentment and defeat.

"We just want you to go to college; after that you can do what you want," said one father.

"I'll never be happy until you get married," a mother told her divorced daughter.

"We think it's time for you to have children," other parents comment.

All these parents mean well, but they are putting expectations on their children, who really want to please them, yet have to be loyal to themselves. Some parents expect their children to settle close by, and when they take employment in another state, parents are likely to resent it.

Once you begin to take inventory, you may be surprised to learn how your attitude and conversation reek with expectations put on yourself and others. Jim and I have been amazed at the expectations we've placed on each other. I'm the worst, since my judgment is emotional. Checking my motivation for doing things for people has helped me to avoid resentment.

Being honest about doing only those things that you feel comfortable doing, and being candid when you feel that others have put unfair expectations on you, requires courage because of the risk that they may be disappointed, upset, even angry and hurt.

Expectations are carried over into church relations where ministers expect people to attend every meeting and agree with all that's being done. Parishioners inflict their expectations when they dictate whether or not their minister's spouse should work, teach classes, or lead groups, and assume that their minister's children should behave better than other children.

The expectations of others are not necessarily God's expectations. We let other people play God when we are tossed around by their expressions of what we think they expect. Many people, especially those with emotional judgment, are susceptible to guilt feelings. Actual guilt is established and confirmed only by Scripture and by violations of God's commandments, not from other people's ultimatums, requests, manipulations, and demands. Finding God's will for our lives is a private trek.

Paul Tournier says that false guilt is brought on from what others say or think—judgments of others. True guilt comes from willfully and knowingly disobeying God.

Our happiness is not the result of manipulating the actions and thoughts of others—that merely feeds our pride. Knowing the difference between healthy pride and false pride relieves resentment and guilt.

Healthy Pride vs. False Pride

False pride pushes us to be something we are not in order to impress or surpass others just to gain recognition. It's a stand-on-a-stack-of-people-so-you-can-see-the-ones-worthy-of-your-attention attitude. False pride criticizes others for what they cannot do or be—noting failures. False pride magnifies its own achievements and abilities, and boasting enters.

False pride puts a whammy on many Christians who berate and ridicule themselves for what they cannot do, assuming the worst, so that perhaps someone will come to the rescue.

The "I gotta be me" philosophy can easily degenerate into self-centered individualism or counterfeit pride, which disregards the goals and needs of others and results in separation and lack of bonding.

Some people wear their so-called humility like a badge—"I'm humble and proud of it." They advertise by declaring, "I'm nothing but a dirt ball"—a nifty cover-up for a feeling of superiority and a sneaky way to avoid failure. The smallest progress is enough.

When we are unduly aware of ourselves or take credit for what we are and can do, that is false pride or egotism in its purest form. Egotism is keeping oneself and one's interests in mind, preoccupation with self, conceit, and superiority. So false pride and egotism are sisters, the brand of pride that is opposite humility and that creeps ever so subtly into our attitudes and out our mouths.

God doesn't regard us as trash; God made us somebodies. God regards us as treasurers, co-workers, and joint heirs. What could be better? Wanting to measure up to someone else is not the name of the game. If we measure ourselves by anyone, it should be Jesus.

Humility and Healthy Pride

What is humility? An action, a position, or an attitude? We might say that a certain person is humbled by problems, lives in a humble dwelling, eats humble pie, and practices humility.

Humility is often regarded as poverty, lack of education, timidity, putting oneself down, withholding personal opinion, embarrassment, mistreating oneself, being a doormat, depriving oneself, or having low self-esteem. But humility and humiliation (shame) are not synonymous.

"Although I pleased my teachers, my mother didn't give me any praise for public speaking because she wanted to keep me humble," Jake said. "When in desperation I'd ask her how I did, she'd say solemnly: 'You weren't the worst, but you weren't the best either.' " Jake's mother meant well, but she had a warped view of humility.

Humility is a lack of pride, modesty, or submission. People ask, "Can you accept yourself, have high self-esteem, and still be humble?" "Can you be assertive and humble at the same time?" The answer is yes, certainly!

Some Christians are so afraid of being proud that they are apt to look down on the gifts and abilities God has given them. They cannot comfortably say thank you after someone compliments them. They feel obligated to say, "Oh, it wasn't very good," or "It could have been much better," or even "I had nothing to do with it." Certainly this attitude can't please the Lord.

Healthy pride means a sense of one's own proper dignity or value, self-respect, pleasure or satisfaction in one's work, achievements, or possessions. Legitimate pride, then, is not negative. God has given us certain capabilities, and when we discount or discredit these inborn abilities and personalities, it constitutes a lack of gratitude to the Giver.

I believe God wants us to be confident in and to accept the way He made us. When we take credit for what we are and what we do, that is false pride. Humility is not a feeling but rather an action, stemming from an attitude of dependence on God. It is one of the healthiest attributes of the human race. Humility involves knowing exactly what we are and how we think, without apologizing or bragging about it. God gave each human being a sense of pride, so when rightly understood, godly pride and humility are companions, not competitors.

Achieving Humility

True humility is recognition that without God we are nothing. With God we are everything He wants us to be—not better than anyone else, but not worse. Therefore, humility is actually achieved by an attitude of respect for ourselves and total dependence on God or reverence for God to provide strength, provisions, enabling, and direction. Allowing God to empower and control our lives expresses humility.

Reading the Bible gives understanding, and praying gives strength and acknowledges our utter dependence on the Lord—which leads to humility. "The fear of the Lord is the beginning of wisdom, and the knowledge of the Holy One is insight" (Prov 9:10). Reverence for God is the beginning and conclusion of the search for meaning to life.

Humility in Action

We cannot get our minds off ourselves until our minds are entwined with the Holy Spirit. "Let the same mind be in you that was in Christ Jesus" (Phil 2:5). Jesus never wavered regarding his mission and position. His walk with God was daily, and his self-respect was healthy. He handled put-downs, rebukes, hatred, and mistreatment, but he was always controlled by God. He believed that "those with good sense are slow to anger, and it is their glory to overlook an offense" (Prov 19:11).

Humility is love in action—Christ on the cross. The Christian life starts a process in which we gradually open our lives to the control of God's spirit. It is our responsibility to yield our wills to God's control each day. This is called walking in the spirit of humility.

We never have humility alone; it is always *with* someone. "Humility is helping the other person become the best person he or she can become, always taking into consideration his or her personal strengths and weaknesses and not putting him or her down or expecting that person to become like you. Submission is synonymous with humility. According to Ephesians 5:21, humility is the basic attitude for all believers: 'Submit to one another out of reverence for Christ.' "[1] Self-esteem is necessary so that we can get our minds off ourselves and onto others to carry out God's command of using our gifts to minister with the strength God provides.

As God's co-workers, our unified goal is to make God's enemies God's friends. Anyone who doesn't know Jesus is God's enemy—not because God made them enemies, but because they have chosen to be enemies or are unaware that they are enemies. Christ invites us as his ambassadors to help make friends for God. This unique plan is revealed in 2 Corinthians 5:18: "All this is from God, who reconciled us to himself through Christ, and has given us the ministry of reconciliation."

Discovering the personal nature of our Creator, His desire to communicate with us, and the way He wants us to cooperate as co-workers is the most thrilling and satisfying lifestyle anyone could imagine, appealing to all types. Jesus said in John 20:21, "As the Father has sent me, so I send you." Until we accept ourselves as Christ accepts us, we cannot realize God's dream and goal of presenting the Good News to every person.

The apostle Peter speaks plainly about what our attitude toward others should be.

> The end of all things is near; therefore be serious and discipline yourselves for the sake of your prayers. Above all, maintain constant love for one

another, for love covers a multitude of sins. . . . Like good stewards of the manifold grace of God, serve one another with whatever gift each of you has received. (1 Pet 4:7, 8, 10)

Finally, all of you, have unity of spirit, sympathy, love for one another, a tender heart, and a humble mind. Do not repay evil for evil or abuse for abuse; but, on the contrary, repay with a blessing. It is for this that you were called—that you might inherit a blessing. (1 Pet 3:8-9)

What is the reason for all this carefulness and humility in action? "In your hearts sanctify Christ as Lord. Always be ready to make your defense to anyone who demands from you an accounting for the hope that is in you" (3:15). We cannot effectively share our faith with others until we recognize our worth before God and accept the way God created us. It is a good thing to have personal confidence, but a better thing to have God-confidence. We have identified the sources of self-esteem in order to use them in true humility.

Now the Lord is the Spirit, and where the Spirit of the Lord is, there is freedom. And all of us, with unveiled faces, seeing the glory of the Lord as though reflected in a mirror, are being transformed into the same image from one degree of glory to another, for this comes from the Lord, the Spirit. (2 Cor 3:17-18)

Conclusion

All the bikers are gathered around the warm campfire, quietly enjoying conversations, one-on-one or in small groups, each patiently listening to the other's ideas, being sensitive to each other's personal need for acceptance and approval. The venture has been worthwhile. Enjoy your trip home!

Thank you, God, for giving us such full and meaningful lives.

Note

[1]Ruth McRoberts Ward, *Appreciation—What Every Woman Still Needs* (Grand Rapids: Baker Book House, 1981) 132.

Afterword

As I reread with a critical eye the first edition of this book, working with pen in hand and making changes, certain impressions came to my mind. I would like to share these with you, arranged by chapters.

Chapter 1

"Confidence comes from knowing who you are and what you can do." These words rang true from a 21-year-old who was brought up on appreciating himself even before he had chosen his career." This young man is now 38, married, and the father of two children. He earned a B.S., M.Div., and Ph.D. and is a professor of philosophy and ethics. And, by the way, he's our youngest son. Knowing and liking who you are and what you like helps in setting goals and keeping your focus.

In the last several years I've concluded that the first step toward developing self-esteem is self-acceptance as God has uniquely designed each person. When we understand ourselves and appreciate how we are different—which is legitimate and okay—then we are positioned to build self-esteem and to accept the ever-present gift of self-esteem that God provides, hopefully in conjunction with the approval and affirmation of others. We (particularly feelers) don't die if we don't receive approval from others—just hurt.

"Being starved for approval and recognition is a common, healthy appetite that some children feel more than others. If children are not served self-esteem, they learn to grab it wherever they can." This idea has been proven repeatedly as I have counseled parents struggling with difficult or overly sensitive children. Seeing parents drastically improve their parenting techniques as they began to understand the dynamics of temperament/type and constructive communication became the major motivation for the book *Coaching Kids: Practical Tips for Effective Communication* (Smyth & Helwys), which Jim and I co-wrote.

"Most people are not even aware of God's unique packaging. Every person possesses neat, built-in, esteem provisions that God designed to form a constant, iron-clad, bottomless reservoir." I love to see the immediate self-acceptance of persons who, when they come into a session don't know who they are by God's design, but leave with renewed appreciation and wonderment that "how I am must be okay." They depart with renewed confidence to repair and sweeten relationships. That mental metamorphous always makes my day!

Chapter 2

"By the time you finish this book, your self-esteem should have increased greatly, and understanding and appreciation of others should also have soared." I wish you could read the letters I've received from readers who have said things such as: "I was ready to take my life until I picked up the *Self-Esteem* book and discovered that I was okay." "My plan was to divorce my husband because he just didn't seem to care about me. Since reading *Self-Esteem* I realize that his temperament is one percent of the nation's and that his needs are totally different from mine. It's not fair for me to expect him to be someone he's not, is it? I've decided to keep him." "I thought something was wrong with our oldest son; he cried about everything. But now I understand that he's a feeler and he'll have to learn to manage that. We'll have to get off his case." These stories verify that these ideas are easily applied.

Chapter 6

"Discovering your child's type will adjust unreal expectations and enable you to release your child to become his or her true self and to pursue a congenial vocation." The family-unit vision hinted at explosive family dynamics when several temperaments are represented, especially with blended families. In counseling families, we became acutely aware of the drastic need for parents and caregivers to give critical attention to understanding temperament and to identifying and destroying the national habitual malady of absent, poor, damaging, and violent dialogue. All this spurred us to combine understanding temperament and healthy dialogue into a tailormade guide for parents—*Coaching Kids: Practical Tips for Effective Communication.*

Chapter 7

Most women make decisions based on feelings, whereas most men make decisions based on thinking. This difference I now call "head logic versus heart logic." It clashes with the general stance in society that all women are or should feel the same and that all men are or should make decisions the same. The resulting resentments, anger and guilt, along with a great need for special understanding and respect for these minority groups, became the major impetus for my writing the book, *Blending Temperaments*. Raising the level of understanding automatically lowers the level of tension. Out of that particular emphasis, three catchy helpful slogans worth memorizing and passing on have emerged:

•Our goal is not to think alike, but to think together.
•Learn to celebrate, not criticize, differences.
•It's difficult to give what you don't need and to withhold what you want to give.

Conclusion

Since I wrote the original *Self-Esteem* book, computers have come to dominate most homes *and* affect temperaments. Intuitives seem to be in love with their computers because they offer a never-ending challenge and plenty of fun. Their spouses will testify to a myriad of reasons why they must have the latest updates on software and how they usually maneuver a way to buy them. Spellcheck protects their reputations—no one will know how they struggle with spelling. Computers can cause marriage problems because many intuitives elect to kiss their computers goodnight.

Many introverts have come alive and gotten in touch with their friends and family through e-mail. They have also discovered their flare for writing and designing stationery and cards. Bored or housebound introverts and extroverts keep the chat rooms buzzing. The Internet has opened a whole new world of personalized communication.

Progress forces sensing people to embrace computers at home and work. Even though they hate changes, sensing people appreciate that in the long run computers are economical, fast, accurate, and neat, but they may not play with them as much as intuitives. They have the patience to learn how to install and service them, thus creating a huge hands-on market. (Good news: Myers-Briggs information, including the questionnaire, can be found on the Internet.)

Healthy self-acceptance/self-esteem is still the key to effective communication, which then leads to wholesome relationships—the serious "bikers" destination. Needless to say, studying self-esteem has directed me down several exciting paths. I trust your self-esteem is hale and hearty, that you are enjoying the challenges of your personal style of biking, and that you are constantly contributing to the self-worth of others.